MICHIGAN STATE UNIVERSITY LIBRARY
AUG 14 2025
WITHDRAWN

 RETURNING MATERIALS:
Place in book drop to remove this checkout from your record. FINES will be charged if book is returned after the date stamped below.

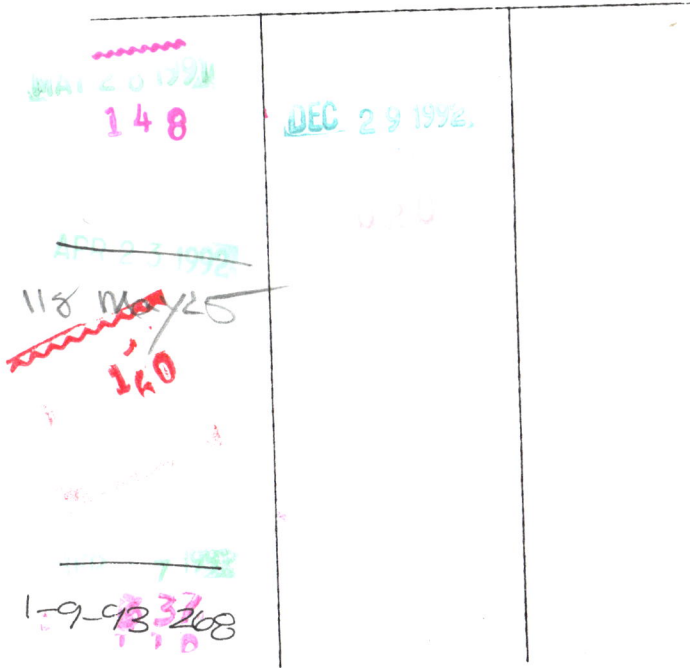

Training Users and Producers in Compiling Statistics and Indicators on Women in Development

United Nations

ST/ESA/STAT/SER.F/45

DEPARTMENT OF INTERNATIONAL ECONOMIC AND SOCIAL AFFAIRS
STATISTICAL OFFICE

ECONOMIC COMMISSION FOR AFRICA
and
INTERNATIONAL RESEARCH AND TRAINING INSTITUTE FOR THE ADVANCEMENT OF WOMEN

STUDIES IN METHODS   Series F   No. 45

TRAINING USERS AND PRODUCERS IN COMPILING STATISTICS AND INDICATORS ON WOMEN IN DEVELOPMENT – Syllabus and related materials from the subregional seminar held in Harare, 29 April to 7 May 1985

UNITED NATIONS
New York, 1987

NOTE

The designations employed and the presentation of the material in this publication do not imply the expression of any opinion whatsoever on the part of the Secretariat of the United Nations concerning the legal status of any country, territory, city or area or of its authorities, or concerning the delimitation of its frontiers or boundaries.

The term "country" as used in the text of this publication also refers, as appropriate, to territories or areas.

The designations "more developed" and "less developed" regions are intended for statistical convenience and do not necessarily express a judgement about the stage reached by a particular country or area in the development process.

ST/ESA/STAT/SER.F/45

UNITED NATIONS PUBLICATION

Sales No. E.87.XVII.6

01700
ISBN 92-1-161284-5

PREFACE

The United Nations International Decade for Women has brought into sharp focus the need for information about women's contribution to development, and it is now widely recognized that existing statistical systems have often failed to provide adequate measures of women's productive as distinguished from their reproductive roles in society. Those who produce national statistics, usually the staff of a central statistical office, must be more sensitive to the need for improved statistics and indicators on women, while among users of those statistics, such as members of women's bureaux, women's units of national political parties and non-governmental organizations, there is need for greater skill and confidence in the interpretation and application of statistics and indicators to policy development and planning. Above all, an ongoing dialogue between the producers and users of statistics and indicators on the situation of women is needed to improve the scope and quality of information available for full integration of women in national development policies and plans, and in planning, monitoring and evaluating development programmes.

In response to the need for improved information and dialogue, the United Nations Economic Commission for Africa (ECA) and the United Nations International Research and Training Institute for the Advancement of Women (INSTRAW), in co-operation with the Statistical Office of the United Nations Secretariat, co-sponsored the Subregional Seminar on Improved Statistics and Indicators for Women in Development. The Seminar was held in Harare, Zimbabwe, from 29 April to 7 May 1985 and was hosted by the Government of Zimbabwe through the Central Statistical Office and the Ministry of Community Development and Women's Affairs. Additional support was provided by the United Nations Fund for Population Activities (UNFPA) and the United Nations Development Fund for Women (UNIFEM). The present document is based on the proceedings of the seminar.

Participants in the Seminar included 38 delegates from 12 countries in eastern and southern Africa, representing both producers and users of statistics and indicators on women, as well as six observers from the host country and eight from national and international organizations. Delegates included both women (21) and men (17) - four women and eight men represented national central statistical offices, while 17 women and nine men represented user organizations. All delegates and observers were invited to participate fully in the activities of the Seminar. Acting as consultant to INSTRAW and the Statistical Office of the United Nations Secretariat, 1/ Jeanne S. Newman served as Technical Co-ordinator of the Seminar and drafted the present report.

The objectives of the Seminar were as follows:

(a) To facilitate a dialogue between producers and users of statistics and indicators on women on sources of data and applications;

1/ Ms. Newman was granted leave to undertake this work through the courtesy of the University Research Corporation, United States of America.

(b) To familiarize participants with:

(i) Sources of data on women;

(ii) The resources of national statistical services;

(iii) A variety of indicators useful for planning, monitoring and evaluating policies, plans and programmes for women in development, together with methods of calculation and presentation;

(iv) Current and potential applications of these indicators;

(v) User organizations;

(c) To provide participants with experience in calculating and presenting a representative set of indicators;

(d) To contribute to the ongoing search for better ways of incorporating data on women into national statistical series and of using such data in policy and programme planning, monitoring and evaluation.

Accordingly, the programme included lectures, participant panels, participatory discussions and programming exercises. As it was intended that the seminar facilitate an exchange of knowledge, experience, information and opinion, every effort was made to involve the delegates as active participants. Delegates served as panelists and as appointed discussants, responding to presentations by the resource staff and participating in general discussion and in small group exercises. They were invited to participate as panelists or discussants for particular topics based upon their specific professional interests, expertise and institutional responsibilities. In this way nearly all delegates were given an opportunity to make specific contributions to the Seminar.

The exercises on demographic, educational, economic and health indicators drew on the 1984 United Nations/INSTRAW publication entitled <u>Compiling Social Indicators on the Situation of Women</u>, 2/ copies of which had been sent to all delegates in advance, and on national materials on women in development gathered for the seminar. The emphasis of the exercises was on the practical aspects of compiling, interpreting and effectively presenting indicators to influence planning and policy development. Sessions were also held on the use of micro-computers for the development and use of data bases on women and for compiling indicators. To help make both the complexity of the data collection activities of central statistical offices and the information needs of user organizations more vivid, a visit to a field office of the Zimbabwe Integrated Household Survey Programme and a women's development project identified by the Ministry of Community Development and Women's Affairs was arranged.

The Seminar was expected to stimulate action at the national level to improve the dialogue between producers and users of statistics, to promote greater sensitivity and creativity on the part of producers in finding ways to provide more

---

2/ United Nations publication, Sales No. E.84.XVII.2.

relevant information to users and to increase skill and confidence on the part of users in obtaining, interpreting and applying statistics and indicators on women, whether provided by national statistical services or obtained from research studies on particular topics. Participants planned to brief their national delegations attending the World Conference to Review and Appraise the Achievements of the United Nations Decade for Women: Equality, Development and Peace, held in Nairobi from 15 to 26 July 1985, about the need for and importance of improved statistics and indicators on the situation of women in development. The participants also recommended that the Seminar sponsors continue to facilitate the exchange of information and seek appropriate channels to bring the concern for better statistics and indicators on women to the attention of the Conference of African Planners, Statisticians and Demographers, which could make recommendations to Governments in the region.

The present publication summarizes the materials considered and the substance of the presentations, panels, general discussion and exercises. Drawing on the experiences described and opinions expressed by users and producers of statistics and indicators in the subregion and reflecting their judgements concerning data needs, availability and constraints, the report is intended, first, to contribute to the ongoing search for improved ways of obtaining and using information on women in development, and second, to offer a potentially useful model to those who may wish to conduct similar seminars in their own countries or in other regions, appropriately adapted to the needs and circumstances in each.

The organization of the report follows that of the Seminar programme and consists of the following major sections:

(a) Review of the demand for, sources and uses of statistics and indicators on women;

(b) Presentation, discussion and computation of statistics and indicators of women's participation in the specific development fields of population structure and change, urbanization and migration, households and families, education and literacy, employment and economic activity, health, women's organizations, and political activity;

(c) Discussion of national programmes for the collection and compilation of statistics on women and for their dissemination and use in national policy and planning;

(d) Exercises to accompany the review of indicators in specific fields.

Comments and requests for further information on the work of the United Nations in this field are welcome. They should be addressed to the Director of the Statistical Office of the United Nations Secretariat, New York, or the Director of the United Nations International Research and Training Institute for the Advancement of Women, Santo Domingo, Dominican Republic.

CONTENTS

Chapter		Page
	Preface	iii
	Explanatory notes	viii
I.	DEMAND FOR AND SOURCES OF STATISTICS AND INDICATORS ON WOMEN	1
	A. Demand for and applications of statistics and indicators on the situation of women	1
	B. Basic data sources	3
	C. Organization of statistical services and their interaction with users	6
II.	STATISTICS AND INDICATORS IN SPECIFIC DEVELOPMENT FIELDS	10
	A. Basic principles for calculating and presenting indicators	11
	B. Population	14
	C. Education, training and literacy	24
	D. Economic activity	32
	E. Health and health services	45
	F. Women's organization	61
	G. Political participation	64
III.	NEEDS AND PROSPECTS FOR IMPROVING STATISTICS AND INDICATORS ON WOMEN IN DEVELOPMENT	67
	A. National programmes	67
	B. Conclusions	71

Exercises

I.	POPULATION	75
II.	EDUCATION	93
III.	ECONOMIC ACTIVITY	104
IV.	HEALTH STATUS, HEALTH SERVICES AND NUTRITION	113

CONTENTS (continued)

Annexes

		Page
I.	OPENING AND CLOSING STATEMENTS	128
II.	LIST OF PARTICIPANTS	129
III.	AIDE MEMOIRE	132
IV.	FIELD VISITS	134
V.	EVALUATION FORM	138
VI.	DOCUMENTS DISTRIBUTED	141

EXPLANATORY NOTES

Symbols of United Nations documents are composed of capital letters combined with figures.

A hyphen (-) between years e.g., 1984-1985, indicates the full period involved, including the beginning and end years; a slash (/) indicates a financial year, academic school year or crop year (e.g., 1984/85).

A point (.) is used to indicate decimals.

The following symbols have been used in tables:

Two dots (..) indicate that data are not available or are not separately reported;

A minus sign (-) before a number indicates a deficit or decrease, except as indicated;

A line (___) indicates data to be filled in as part of the student exercises.

Details and percentages in tables and figures do not necessarily add up to totals, because of rounding.

Data contained in the exercises are for illustrative purposes only. For official data, the sources cited in the tables should be consulted.

I. DEMAND FOR AND SOURCES OF STATISTICS AND INDICATORS ON WOMEN

(First day of the programme)

Following an introduction on the origins, purposes and organization of the Seminar by the Director of the Zimbabwe Central Statistical Office, Gibson Mandishona, the first day was devoted to a discussion of the demand for and sources of national statistics and indicators on women, under the following three topics:

(a) The demand for and application of statistics and indicators on the situation of women;

(b) Basic sources for statistics and indicators on women;

(c) The organization of statistical services and their interaction with users.

For each of these topics, a similar format was used. The subject was introduced in one or two 10- to 20-minute prepared presentations by resource staff. The introduction was followed by the comments of one or more discussants who had previously been selected from among the delegates; the invited comments were followed, time permitting, by general discussion. At the start of the afternoon session, the Technical Co-ordinator, Jeanne Newman, summarized the main points made in the morning session and gave an overview of the afternoon programme. This pattern of review and overview at the start of each session was used throughout the programme.

A. Demand for and applications of statistics and indicators on the situation of women

The topic was introduced by the representative of the International Training and Research Institute for the Advancement of Women (INSTRAW), Mervat Tellawy. She traced the development of international demand for improved statistics and indicators on women to assist countries in planning for the full integration of women into social and economic development. A need for better information to highlight differentials in the situation of women and men was expressed early in the 1970s, and the World Conference of the International Women's Year, held in Mexico City in 1975, had emphasized that need in its Plan of Action. As a result, INSTRAW had undertaken the task of helping to increase knowledge in that area, focusing its efforts on development issues and on the information concerning women needed to facilitate their contribution to development.

Accordingly, INSTRAW and the Statistical Office of the United Nations Secretariat had prepared two United Nations publications of special relevance to this task. The first, Compiling Social Indicators on the Situation of Women 1/ was primarily concerned with effective utilization of statistics currently available in many countries to develop reliable indicators on the situation of women from censuses, household surveys and registration systems. It suggested ways of

---

1/ United Nations publication, Sales No. E.84.XVII.2.

generating basic indicators about women from these data using current concepts and data collection methods.

The second publication, <u>Improving Concepts and Methods for Statistics and Indicators of the Situation of Women</u> 2/ critically reviewed the concepts and methods most widely used in ongoing national data collection programmes. It suggested possible strategies for modifying existing international recommendations for these programmes to collect more adequate and unbiased statistics on women's roles in development. In addition, beginning with the Harare Seminar, the first of its kind, INSTRAW was taking the lead in organizing meetings at the international, regional and national levels to bring together both producers and users of information on women in development to consider how best to improve those statistics and indicators.

In the second half of the introduction, Wilfred Tichagwa (Zimbabwe), focused on specific issues concerning information needs, demands and applications in countries. In Zimbabwe, for example, the Ministry of Community Development and Women's Affairs had recognized its need for adequate statistics on women, in particular rural women, beginning with a review of the situation in which women had found themselves at independence, when they were oppressed both by the white minority rulers and by the traditional patriarchal society. Independence had found a grossly underdeveloped population, largely rural and very poor, in which women were the most disadvantaged group. To change the situation, the Ministry was created to foster self-help, self-reliance and the full participation of women, in particular rural women, in development. The Ministry had four major areas of activity:

(a) Promoting positive changes in the existing legal system, for example, supporting recent successful efforts to establish age 18 as the legal age of majority for both women and men;

(b) Promoting income-generating projects at the community level;

(c) Promoting social development projects, such as pre-school programmes for 0- to 6-year-olds. Such programmes were intended to improve the physical and mental well-being of children and to prepare them for formal education while releasing time for their mothers to improve their own productivity. A second example was an adult literacy programme carried out in co-operation with the Ministry of Education;

(d) Developing infrastructure, such as feeder roads, bridges, safe wells, club halls and primary health care (PHC).

To carry out those activities, the Ministry needed adequate statistics and indicators for planning programmes and services in such areas as:

(a) The number of 0- to 6-year-olds in particular areas to assess needs for and coverage of pre-school programmes;

(b) The number of women who were within walking distance of a PHC clinic or were served by each village health worker (VHW), or who had access to a nearby

---

2/ United Nations publication, Sales No. E.84.XVII.3.

supply of clean water, to assess the availability and accessibility of primary health care and plan for improved coverage;

(c) The number of women in unregistered traditional marriages who might thus face inheritance problems if widowed.

There was also a pressing need for statistics at the community level. The Ministry's research unit, only two years old, had not yet been able to carry out much statistical analysis and, indeed, did not always know what data were already available through the Central Statistical Office or other statistical services. Their current use of statistics was weak but their potential demand for statistics was high.

In reviewing national experience, the discussants for the topic, Gladys Mulindi (Kenya) and F. Chatsalira (Malawi), stressed the need to mobilize and educate women at the grass-roots level so that they might increase their self-reliance and improve their living standards. The consequent need for information at the community level to assist local groups of women in project planning and evaluation was also pointed out. In Kenya, non-governmental organizations had assisted projects in the areas of energy, water supply, nutrition, family planning, primary health care, agricultural production and income-generation. Often, however, participants in those projects did not have the information they needed to gauge the market for the output of their products, and consequently, the projects would not be viable. Nor did non-governmental organizations always have the necessary information about existing projects, national and community needs and trends to provide adequate advice. The non-governmental organizations were hopeful that the new Kenya government programme to organize development at the district level would result in the greater availability of district-level data and thus improve their ability to assist their member groups.

In Malawi there was similarly a high demand for data on women for development planning. For example, data on illiteracy, which in Malawi was higher among women than among men, were used to plan and administer a national literacy programme. Moreover, in response to statistics on university enrolment, a concerted effort was under way to increase the enrolment of women in the scientific and technological disciplines.

B. Basic data sources

Toma J. Makannah, a representative of the Economic Commission for Africa, introduced the topic of basic data sources. He described the three main sources of national data: censuses, sample surveys and administrative records. The current status of those data systems in the participating countries was reviewed and concrete illustrations were provided of some of the tabulations on the situation of women which data from these sources made possible, using census data as an example.

The national population census was a major source of data on women, provided that tabulations were produced for both sexes. Because the census covered the entire population, census statistics could also be reliably compiled for relatively small geographical areas and for specific sub-populations. Many African countries had already conducted two or three national censuses and had acquired considerable experience in census work. Moreover, all African countries had agreed to publish census tabulations by sex. However, as a national population census was taken only infrequently, usually every 10 years, was expensive to conduct and was a time-consuming process, the level of detail on particular topics must be limited and the data might be obsolete well before the next census. Sample surveys were therefore the key both to inter-censal data and to more detailed information on specific topics.

In Africa, the Economic Commission for Africa and the Statistical Office of the United Nations were assisting countries in developing systematic national household survey programmes. Under the African National Household Survey Capability Programme, national statistical services were assisted in organizing their survey programmes to make use of a permanent, well-trained field staff to investigate a series of topics, such as agriculture, labour force, household expenditures and nutrition, using, for example, systematic rotation. Such programmes were yielding a wealth of detailed information on important development issues, most of which should be available separately for each sex. Because information was obtained only from a sample of the population, however, those data were not usually available for small areas, although rural and urban breakdowns were generally possible.

All government ministries maintained administrative records, as did parastatals, private firms, universities and research institutes, and they were often important sources of data, again provided that the records were maintained separately by sex. Small-scale studies and those studies using anthropological and other non-traditional methods of data collection were available to supplement information from the three major sources.

Finally, Mr. Makannah noted that although the three major data sources had different advantages and disadvantages, they were complementary. Accordingly, it was important that they use common concepts, definitions and classifications as much as possible so that analysts could use data from more than one source and be confident that the data were generally compatible.

User organizations should take an active role in suggesting topics to include in censuses and surveys, but as those were costly undertakings and there were competing interests among potential users of data, requests for additional information on women must clearly state the ways in which such data were to be used.

The three major sources of data also had certain shortcomings for obtaining information on women. Sex-based stereotypes and cultural preconceptions might affect survey design and questionnaire formulation. For example, the assumption that most women were not in the labour force had influenced the way in which questions on economic activity were worded; surveys therefore failed to record much of the economic work most women did. There were also biases in the collection, processing, compilation and tabulation of data. Female births and deaths or participation in the labour force were frequently under-reported, older ages were often ascribed to very young married women, and tabulations on the labour force, especially by occupation and industry, were frequently published only for males or were not tabulated by sex. International efforts were under way to try to refine the more troublesome concepts, such as household head and economic activity, to eliminate bias as much as possible. The African National Household Survey Capability Programme was a mechanism to obtain better data on women, particularly on women's economic activities and their role in the informal sector.

Additional discussion on this topic followed four themes which recurred throughout the programme:

(a) Problems with existing concepts and data collection methodologies for national data;

(b) The importance of detailed small-area data and innovative ways to obtain it;

(c) The need for special studies to supplement traditional, national sources;

(d) The need for dialogue between producers and users of national data and the responsibility of producers to disseminate information rapidly and widely.

On problems with existing concepts and methodologies, the following points were noted:

(a) It might be difficult to obtain information on the informal sector from either censuses or surveys for activities which were illegal;

(b) It was important in survey design to identify the appropriate respondent, that is, the most important person in the household, to answer a given set of questions;

(c) There might be a continuing sex bias in the assignment of the two sexes to the categories "own-account worker" and "unpaid family worker", as in the following example: a woman independently produces yarn and her husband weaves that yarn into cloth; he is counted as an own-account worker and she his helper, though both meet the definition of "own-account worker";

(d) There were problems with the concept of household and household head in many countries. Countries defined those in different ways and no one way appeared to be universal. A classification of household types had been proposed for Europe and typologies relevant to other regions were needed.

On small area data and ways to obtain it, the following points were noted:

(a) The need for small area information should be re-emphasized and national experience considered. For example, a pilot village register scheme was being tested in two regions in the United Republic of Tanzania to improve administrative record systems at the village level. For each cell of 10 households a register was maintained by a designated member of one of the households, containing information on persons by sex and age, school enrolment, adult participation in village life, housing and sanitary conditions, number of 25-year-olds with "Road-to-Health" charts, child nutrition status, births, deaths and moves. Quarterly summaries from each of the 10 household cells provided the village leaders with periodic village profiles. A compilation was to be made annually at the regional level. As the scheme was still in the pilot stage, no evaluation had yet been made of either the accuracy of the data or the cost of the system;

(b) Geographical boundaries of administrative districts often differed from ministry to ministry, making the use of district-level administrative statistics from more than one ministry difficult;

(c) Competition for financial resources made it difficult to amass all the data, particularly small area data, that users wanted.

On the topic of special research studies, the usefulness of small, specialized, detailed studies to learn about such issues as agricultural decision-making within the household and the need to be creative in developing appropriate methodologies for those studies were stressed.

The need for interaction between producers and users of statistics and indicators on women and for producers to take the initiative in disseminating the results of surveys widely and rapidly was also reiterated. For example, users in Botswana played a key role in helping to design the 1981 census. Because of user demand for housing information there, the census became one of population and housing and not of population alone.

C. Organization of statistical services and their interaction with users

David Mzite (Zimbabwe) introduced the topic of organization of statistical services and their interaction with users. Questions to be addressed in this field included the following:

(a) Given the many competing and changing demands of user organizations for information, what was the best way of meeting them?

(b) Who should be supported to produce those data - the ministries themselves? The central statistical office?

(c) To what extent should the activities of central statistical offices be decentralized to meet user needs more effectively?

In Zimbabwe, prior to independence the Central Statistical Office had not concerned itself with data on the population as a whole. The focus had been on males working in the formal sector. Consequently, virtually no data existed for 80 per cent of the population, and what little existed were out of date, as they were gathered in 1969. The Central Statistical Office itself was highly centralized. At independence, the immediate question had been how best to organize to obtain the essential baseline data on the entire population as quickly as possible. In 1981, a national committee had been set up to design the questionnaire for a national census, but as most ministries had no information for planning, they all wanted detailed data in their areas of responsibility at once. As that would have been impossible, it had been decided instead to conduct a simple one-page census of general demographic and housing characteristics immediately, and then search for other means of obtaining more detailed information in these and other areas.

Late in 1981, a co-ordinating body from all the ministries had been set up to look at the areas where information was required, identify a set of key indicators and establish priorities for data collection. The Central Statistical Office had decided to participate in the African National Household Survey Capability Programme, and in 1982 it had set up a permanent survey unit with field offices and established a schedule of surveys in accordance with the priorities identified. Because information on agriculture, in particular peasant agriculture, was a high priority, agricultural surveys were carried out annually. In 1981 a manpower survey had been carried out; in 1983/84 demographic and socio-economic surveys had been carried out; and an income, consumption and expenditure survey was under way in 1984/85. Other topics to follow were: labour force (1985/86), literacy (1985/86), and inter-censal demographic survey (1986/87). Most of the information women need would eventually be covered, but the Central Statistical Office must first build its own capability for conducting decentralized surveys, learning from experience how many surveys they could handle in a year and how quickly they could produce the data.

To carry out its ambitious programme, the Central Statistical Office was organized into two divisions: the Economic Statistics Division, which provided information on national accounts, agricultural production, prices and finance; and the Social and Population Statistics Division, with responsibility for censuses, surveys, vital registration and the like. Data collection was decentralized to field offices. Because resources were limited, the Central Statistical Office and the ministries had developed a co-operative strategy for surveys on energy use, water and sanitation, contraceptive prevalence and health/nutrition status. The relevant ministries channelled resources to the Central Statistical Office for data collection, while data processing, analysis and publication were carried out by the ministries themselves with assistance as appropriate from the Central Statistical Office. The Office maintained a copy of the data and was building up a national data base. At the moment, there were no special problems at the data collection level, but there were delays in processing the data through the government computer centre, which must serve all departments.

It was also noted that the pre-independence vital registration system in Zimbabwe, which had never covered the entire population, was experiencing serious difficulties. Although the Central Statistical Office realized the importance of the system, particularly to the Ministry of Health, it could not yet give its restructuring priority.

The Central Statistical Office did not always know who, beyond the government ministries, the users were, what data users wanted or how the data would be used. Users changed and their needs and demands changed. A mechanism for ongoing dialogue was therefore essential. To facilitate the dialogue, Zimbabwe was to hold a large conference of producers and users of data in 1986.

From the standpoint of users of statistics and indicators on women, a central statistical office could meet the need for the following kinds of information:

    (a) Basic background information on the situation of women;

    (b) Key policy-relevant indicators on women;

    (c) Timely statistics;

    (d) Data at the small area or community level;

    (e) An inventory of what data on women are available.

Also needed were mechanisms to obtain statistics on phenomena which were not part of the regular national data collection programme.

Users must be aware of factors affecting the availability of such statistics from a central statistical office, such as limited resources, competing demands, burdensome workloads, the strength and organization of a country's statistical infrastructure and the degree of its centralization or decentralization. However, users must also become aware of the potential uses of existing data and take the initiative in requesting data. The critical importance of developing mechanisms to facilitate co-ordination and an ongoing dialogue at all stages - data collection design, analysis, tabulation and use - must be emphasized. Because the sources of data on women were as varied as the users, it was important that Central Statistical Offices play a strong role in the co-ordination. A good example was the experience of Zimbabwe in using a co-ordinating committee to select and schedule survey topics. Women's groups should be an important part of such committees.

Discussants for the topic were Susan Yoyo (Zambia) and D. O. Ahawo (Kenya). Mechanisms currently being used in countries to facilitate communication between producers and users of statistics on women were reviewed in the discussion.

In Zambia, for example, the strategy of the United Independence Party (UNIP) was to improve national policies affecting women through co-operation in gathering and analysing information on women between the Central Statistical Office, the Research Bureau of UNIP and a wide variety of operating agencies. Because the Central Statistical Office must respond to a variety of demands with limited staff and resources, the Party had established its own Research Bureau to supplement information available from the Office with the results of special analyses of existing data and other technical research relevant to policy-making. Technical assistance to the Research Bureau of UNIP was provided by the Central Statistical Office. In 1983, on the recommendation of the Women's Affairs Committee, which advised the Central Committee on policy issues affecting women, data analysis and technical research on women in development had been added to the Bureau's research agenda.

To supplement its own limited staff, the Research Bureau had developed a strategy to involve the operating agencies of the Government, parastatals, and trade unions and other non-governmental organizations in research on issues of significance to women. A liaison committee of the participating organizations met with Research Bureau and the staff of the Central Statistical Office to agree on the type of information needed and on the specific data to be collected from each institution. Each agency also designated a liaison person who was responsible for collecting the desired information from her/his own institution and for forwarding it to the professional staff of the Research Bureau for analysis. The Women's Affairs Committee then used the research results in advising the Central Committee of UNIP on the relevant policies and plans. Although there had been some problems, particularly in controlling the quality of the data, the response had been overwhelmingly positive.

The Kenya Central Bureau of Statistics had an ongoing programme to provide policy-makers, planners and the public with continuous social and economic information about the population. Currently, efforts were being made to decentralize both development planning and the collection and analysis of the data on which that planning must be based.

The Social Statistics Section of the Bureau had a programme of continuous and _ad hoc_ household surveys on a variety of subjects, including the situation of women and children. Specific attention to statistics on women began in 1977 with the publication of Women in Kenya, and that attention had continued. In 1984, the Bureau had published Situation Analysis of Women and Children in Kenya, and it was producing two volumes of data on women at the provincial level. A country profile had been prepared for the World Conference to Review and Appraise the Achievements of the United Nations Decade for Women, held at Nairobi in 1985.

Currently, with the Government's decision to make development planning a responsibility of district planning officers, who knew their districts' situation well, the Bureau was trying to prepare a statistical report for each of the 42 districts. Those reports were expected to include information at the district level on the situation of women. To determine what information was needed for those reports, the Bureau had to go to the local population.

Overall, though large amounts of data were produced in Kenya, it was not always easy for the Bureau to know what tabulations would be most useful for its users, who were becoming more sophisticated. Better dialogue and perhaps a round table of producers and users at all levels was needed. In addition, because of the volume of data the Bureau produced reports more slowly than was desirable. It might be that data processing and analysis should also be decentralized by using microcomputers.

Five issues were considered in the discussion:

(a) What mechanisms could ensure input by users into decisions on what data a central statistical office should gather and tabulate?

(b) What difficulties did a central statistical office encounter in identifying who the relevant users were?

(c) What mechanisms could ensure that information on women was given priority in the ongoing data collection programme of a central statistical office?

(d) What special problems were there in obtaining adequate information on women in the rural and non-formal sectors?

(e) What difficulties were associated with involving the ministries and other user organizations in data collection?

With respect to the last issue, two problems were stressed: first, the often uneven quality of the data collected by users who were inexperienced in statistics, and second, the frequent resistance of ministries and operating agencies to any change in the way they had always maintained their records. Since there was some justification for such resistance, in any given situation the trade-offs between continuity and responsiveness to change must be negotiated. With respect to data quality, it was suggested that liaison persons in each co-operating ministry or agency be trained in elementary statistics and that strong links be maintained between those persons and the Central Statistical Office.

II. STATISTICS AND INDICATORS IN SPECIFIC DEVELOPMENT FIELDS

(Second through fifth days of the programme)

Having considered the demand for and sources of statistics and indicators on women, the participants turned their attention to the identification, definition, calculation, interpretation and presentation of specific development statistics and indicators. To introduce the discussion of those indicators, the conceptual framework presented during the introductory session was reviewed in more detail and basic principles for calculating and presenting indicators were outlined. Following those presentations and general discussion, specific statistical series were described, discussed and calculated in five broad development areas: (a) population structure and change; (b) education and literacy; (c) economic activity; (d) health and nutrition; and (e) organization and political participation.

Full participation was stressed. Each topic within a specific development area was introduced through a presentation by one or two members of the resource team or by a panel of participant presenters. Resource team presentations were followed in most instances by brief comments from designated discussants. Opportunity was also provided for general discussion of each topic or groups of topics. Finally, for each broad development area, participants were divided into four small working groups, each with a resource staff member as facilitator, to undertake a series of exercises in extracting, interpreting and presenting statistics and indicators on women's situation from commonly available data. These exercises are reproduced in a separate section below.

The objectives of the exercises were as follows:

(a) Through the examination of data collection instruments and published tabulations, to provide participants with experience in <u>identifying</u> those indicators which might usefully be extracted from an existing data set;

(b) To provide participants with experience in <u>calculating</u> illustrative statistics and indicators on the situation of women;

(c) Through exercises in <u>interpreting</u> statistics calculated from tabulations, to sensitize participants to the importance of understanding how data were collected and what the limitations and levels of uncertainty were in the statistics and indicators calculated from those data;

(d) Through the construction of tables, graphs and charts, to familiarize participants with several ways of <u>presenting</u> statistics and indicators for effective communication with policy-makers and planners.

Each participant was furnished an inexpensive hand calculator to use in completing the exercises. Exercises on a given topic were handed out the day before that topic was discussed. Participants were assigned to groups simply by counting off around the table. The procedure ensured that the groups were of approximately of equal size and were heterogeneous with respect to country and professional experience. In each of the groups, experienced statisticians assisted their colleagues with less quantitative experience in extracting statistics and indicators and in performing calculations, while those whose expertise lay more in policy development and programme planning took the lead in interpretation and presentation. Only one and one-half hours had been allowed each day (days 2-5) for the small group exercises, and since several exercises had been prepared for each of the four areas (population, education, economic activity, health), participants were not expected to complete every exercise. They were encouraged instead to take home those they had not finished for completion later.

A. Basic principles for calculating and presenting indicators

1. A conceptual framework for construction of development indicators

In introducing the consideration of specific indicators, Mr. Mandishona (Zimbabwe) began by tracing the growth of interest in devising a measure which, unlike the macro-economist's GNP or GDP, would give emphasis to the social dimensions of development. He stressed that a desirable system of development indicators must reflect a country's development goals and should be structured to permit disaggregation by:

(a) Geographical levels (national, regional, local);

(b) Subject-matter dimensions (social, economic, political);

(c) Social groups sub-systems (ethnic, socio-economic);

(d) Population classifications (age, sex, location).

Indicators should point to progress towards or retreat from desired socio-economic goals and should provide signals for action.

He reviewed a number of problems with existing social indicator systems. The first problem lay in the ad hoc nature of most systems. Not having arisen from an adequate theory of social structure and change, most were lists of specific indicators developed in response to requests for particular information. Other problems included poor statistical terminology and inadequate data, structural problems, a large informal and non-monetarized sector complicating collection and analysis of data, problems of measurement and scaling, and so on. In general, objective indicators were preferable to subjective ones, and simple indicators to composites. In the social indicator movement there was as yet no "total progress" indicator that was comparable to gross domestic product as an overall economic indicator.

The improvement of data systems and the information base was an integral part of general development and should itself be monitored in any system of development indicators. The system should also include indicators of population, education, health and nutrition, housing, income, expenditure, consumption and the national economy. In accordance with the goals enunciated in the Lagos Plan of Action, [3]

---

[3] The Lagos Plan of Action for the Implementation of the Monrovia Strategy for the Economic Development of Africa was adopted at the second extraordinary meeting of Heads of State and Government of the Organization of African Unity, held at Lagos in April 1980.

the system should monitor progress towards distributive social justice, the provision of basic needs and growth in GDP. To those ends high priority should be given to monitoring the following:

(a) Short-term economic performance;

(b) Agricultural productivity;

(c) Human resource development (health, employment, education and manpower);

(d) The participation of women in the economy.

A list of specific indicators which might be included in a system to monitor those key sectors was introduced. The indicators were grouped into five categories: basic needs, population participation, national security, economic performance and population phenomena. The importance of presenting the indicators separately for rural and urban populations was stressed.

In subsequent discussions the categorization of indicators was referred to several times. Several participants noted that the suggested measures appeared to have an urban bias. Others also suggested that the focus of the category on population participation was on participation outside the home and did not address the problems of rural women. In rural areas, participation involved decision-making within the household about what to do, when to do it and who should do it. Males usually made those decisions even when they no longer resided in the rural areas. There appeared to be general agreement that although it was unlikely that a definitive list could be developed, countries should develop their own framework based on a coherent view of the country's developed goals, as the presentation had emphasized. The listing presented in that paper was a useful place to begin.

2. Principles for developing indicators of the situation of women

The topic was introduced by Grace Bediako and the Technical Co-ordinator, Ms. Newman. The seminar reviewed three major objectives in the selection of indicators on the situation of women:

(a) To show differentials between women and men;

(b) To show how the differentials change over time;

(c) To monitor the impact of certain policies on the differentials.

In developing and interpreting a set of indicators once the subject to be monitored has been decided on, a number of questions must be addressed, including the following:

(a) What type of indicator is to be calculated?

(i) <u>Numbers</u>, for example, the number of persons falling into a given category. This is an absolute not a relative measure and therefore does not measure differentials;

(ii) <u>Proportions</u>, for example, the number of persons in a given category as a proportion of all persons (when multiplied by 100, a proportion becomes a percentage of the total);

(iii) <u>Ratios</u>, for example, the number of persons in a given category divided by the number of persons in another category;

(iv) <u>Rates</u>, for example, the number of persons in a given category as a proportion of all persons who <u>could</u> be in (that is, who are at risk for) that category;

The numerator in each case may be the same but the denominator will differ, and it is the denominator which is key to interpretation of the statistics;

(b) What framework will be used for comparisons? Will the basis of analysis be the population as a whole or some subgroup based on other characteristics, such as age, marital status or educational attainment?

(c) How can one decide whether female/male differentials are significant? Standard statistical tests for differences between group means, medians or percentages are used to determine the significance of differentials between women and men;

(d) What are the reasons for these differentials? The answer to this question generally lies outside the indicator itself. It is often necessary to carry out a separate in-depth study to determine the reasons for differentials.

The Co-ordinator stressed that, from all the possible indicators one could list, the specific set chosen for monitoring should consist of those most relevant to that country's situation, that is, those reflecting its most critical national problems, those most likely to change during that country's development and those likely to have differential impacts on the women and men of the country. For that reason, although most countries would seek information on the same broad development areas, they would differ in the specific set of statistics and indicators selected for monitoring.

She suggested a number of guidelines for constructing indicators on women in development:

(a) Use existing national data series wherever possible, noting their deficiencies and supplementing them with special studies where feasible;

(b) Construct indicators of broad applicability;

(c) Develop indicators which are both valid and reliable measures for the phenomena of interest;

(d) Develop indicators which reflect the participation of women in all aspects of development;

(e) Develop indicators which describe the situation of women relative to that of men;

(f) Develop indicators which are easily interpreted and are signals to action;

(g) As no single indicator can capture women's many roles, avoid composite indexes. They are hard to interpret and may obscure important differentials;

(h) Present statistics and indicators in simple tables and graphically where possible.

B. Population

1. Population composition and growth

The Technical Co-ordinator introduced the discussion of indicators of population structure and change by noting that the situation of women could not be considered apart from the general social and economic conditions prevailing in the country. Some countries had large populations, others had small. Some were densely populated, others had widely scattered populations. Some had highly mobile populations, whether as a result of labour mobility, refugee flight or nomadic circulation; others were more settled. In Africa, although all countries were primarily rural, most were urbanizing rapidly. All African countries had young populations and high dependency ratios, that is, the ratio of those under age 15 and over age 64 to those of working ages (15-64). Many were culturally, ethnically and religiously diverse. Those demographic variations, she said, affected the situation of women in different and sometimes unexpected ways.

She pointed out that the distribution of the population by age and sex defined a pool of potential candidates for life stage and gender-defined activities. Accordingly, indicators describing that distribution were fundamental. Of those, the most basic was the sex ratio, that is, the number of males for each 100 females in the population. The usual range was between 90 and 103 males per 100 females, but the ratio differed by age and usually by rural/urban residence. Where it was very low, as in Botswana, where it was only 85 in the 1981 census, that was rarely due to mortality differentials but rather to the semi-permanent or temporary out-migration of young males seeking employment elsewhere.

The Co-ordinator briefly described the age distribution characteristics of countries in different stages of demographic development. Countries with high fertility and mortality had age distributions shaped like a pyramid, with each successively younger cohort larger than the preceding. Countries with low fertility and mortality régimes, and therefore with lower rates of growth, had age distributions shaped like a gradually tapering column. Transition from high fertility and mortality régimes to low was reflected in a bulging, tree-shaped distribution.

Grouping the population into broad age groups within which most were at approximately similar life stages provided a convenient way to summarize the age distribution. Age groupings commonly used were:

(a) Infants and young children: aged 0-4;

(b) Children: aged 5-14;

(c) Youth: aged 15-24;

(d) Adults: aged 25-44 and 45-59;

   (e) Elderly: aged 60 and over.

Within each country, modified and more detailed groupings were often required for work in specific fields.

   Because of the higher female expectation of life at birth in nearly all countries, the male age distribution was generally shifted somewhat towards the younger ages relative to that of women. Sex ratios in the individual 5- or 10-year age groups were subject to large errors due to age misreporting and were highly variable.

   The Co-ordinator mentioned that one useful indicator of the overall age distribution was the dependency ratio, which was the sum of those under 5 and those age 65 and over, divided by those of working age, that is, 15-64. Although not everyone under 5 or over 64 was dependent and not everyone aged 15-64 was able to work, the ratio served as a rough indicator of how many persons each active adult must support. The child/woman ratio provided similar information. It was defined as the number of children under age 5 divided by the number of women of reproductive age and pointed to the average child-care burden of each woman.

   The Co-ordinator noted that the specific demographic processes of birth, death and movement of people were responsible for the age and sex distribution of a population and its increase or decrease. Although these were to be considered in later sessions, she briefly described the calculation of several measures of fertility and of mortality. She pointed out that such measures differed primarily in their choice of denominator to reflect as adequately as possible those "at risk" for the births or deaths included in the numerator. Fertility, for example, could be measured as:

   (a) Crude birth rate: number of births in a given year divided by total mid-year population (x 1000);

   (b) General fertility rate: number of births in a given year divided by mid-year female population aged 15-49 (x 1000);

   (c) Age-specific fertility rates: Number of births in a given year to women of a specific age group divided by mid-year number of women of that age group (x 1000).

Because populations at different levels of social and economic development had characteristic patterns of fertility and mortality, crude birth and death rates (CBR and CDR) could serve as rough general indicators of the situation of women, as could the difference between the two, the crude rate of natural increase (CRNI).

   The Co-ordinator closed by warning that cross-national comparisons might not always be valid because countries frequently used age groups which differed from the now-classic five-year groups. Moreover, countries differed in degrees of age misreporting and under-reporting of certain age and sex groups. In Africa, it was often the women who were not reported or whose ages were unknown. In the United States, the Bureau of the Census appeared to be unable to find and count all the young black males, who showed up in later censuses, after they had reached age 25.

The discussant for the presentation on indicators of population structure, Harish Bundhoo (Mauritius), made the following points:

(a) Decreasing dependency burden was not necessarily a positive indicator for development if many of the larger numbers in the working ages did not have employment and if the country could not afford the increased costs of old-age pensions;

(b) Because of higher rural-urban migration of young males, the age-sex distribution in urban areas was affected more by migration than by fertility and mortality;

(c) Since changes in the age structure with development tended to favour women, unless those women had greater access to economic activity, the society would face increasing need to care for widows;

(d) Finally, the interpretation of indicators was not always obvious. In many areas female participation in the labour force was increasing, but that did not necessarily imply that the situation of women was improving. In countries with high unemployment, if female labour costs were low, as was usually the case, women often moved from the household to the industrial sector. Wages and working conditions might deteriorate for women while men remained unemployed.

2. Population distribution, migration and urbanization

Mr. Makannah (Economic Commission for Africa) introduced the discussion of statistics and indicators of population mobility and distribution by emphasizing that such indicators should be selected to help Africa deal with the two major issues of distribution:

(a) A very uneven population distribution across the continent;

(b) A rapidly increasing urban population, even while the bulk of the population was rural. Urban population growth was the result of both high fertility and migration.

He noted that it was particularly important to improve statistics on the levels, trends, causes and consequences of migration and urbanization for women. First, basic indicators were needed, currently and over time, on the urbanization of women, including:

(a) Proportion of the urban population who were women, by age;

(b) Proportion of urban migrants who were women, by age;

(c) Sizes of the cities to which people were moving, by sex.

Beyond the basic statistics, indicators were also needed to help identify the proximate causes and consequences of urbanization to guide policy and action. To what extent were cities growing as a result of migration? Of fertility? To answer that question, statistics were needed on:

(a) Percentage of migrants in each city, by duration of residence, sex and age;

(b) Fertility of women in urban areas, by length of urban residence and age.

Were the cities able to provide facilities and services to their residents and particularly to women? To answer that question, statistics were needed by size of city on:

(a) Unemployment by sex among young school leavers;

(b) Employment of migrants by sex;

(c) Among employed women, the percentage employed in cities and in given industries;

(d) The proportion of urban households headed by women, among migrants and non-migrants;

(e) The proportion of urban women who had access to hospitals, schools, credit, and the like.

What were the consequences of urban migration to the sending regions, that is, the areas of origin? Statistics on rural as well as urban population were needed on:

(a) Age and sex distribution;

(b) Fertility, by age;

(c) Unemployment of school leavers, by sex;

(d) Employment and industry, by sex;

(e) Access to social and economic facilities and services, by sex;

(f) Proportion of households headed by women.

Other questions could be addressed. What were the consequences of labour mobility to other countries? What happened to production of goods and services when men left the country? To family formation and social relationships? Indicators were the first step in understanding the causes and consequences of migration and urbanization.

The first discussant for the topic was Celestina Ssewankambo (Zambia). She reviewed issues of population mobility and distribution in Zambia. She pointed out that during colonial days migration and urbanization had been primarily male phenomena. As a result, sex ratios had been very uneven in rural and urban areas. The situation had changed in recent years, so that by 1980, urban sex ratios had been close to unity. Indeed, in some urban areas the numbers of women exceeded those of men. Ms. Ssewankambo suggested that the increased female urban migration evident in Zambia might be due to improvements in female education and consequently in employment opportunities for women in urban areas.

She noted that Zambia had relatively high levels of urbanization (35 per cent of the total population) and a very unevenly distributed population. Fully 22 per cent of the population lived in the copper belt, almost all of which was urbanized, while another 4 per cent lived in Lusaka. Urban populations were currently growing at a rate of 6.7 per cent per year, a rate which was slightly more than 2 percentage points lower than it had been at independence. The slow-down in the rate of urban growth was the result of deliberate public policy. To encourage people to return to rural areas, the Government had instituted programmes to disperse industries to rural areas and to stimulate the growth of district centres.

N. Mbere (Botswana) reported on a 1980 survey which showed that many of the women who migrated to urban areas ended up in low-wage employment as domestics or worked in the informal sector at activities, such as beer brewing, which were not economically viable. Rural women also migrated as agricultural labourers. They too were easily exploited. They usually received low wages, were not entitled to other benefits and were dismissed when they became pregnant. The survey also found that because of male labour migration, more than 40 per cent of households were headed by women. Many of those women had little access to land, labour, credit or other economic resources. Rural-to-urban migrants reported moving in stages: from rural areas to small towns to larger towns and then to cities. The Government of Botswana had instituted policies to encourage them to remain in the smaller and medium-sized towns.

In the general discussion, the following points were made:

(a) Several countries were concerned about slowing down their rates of urban growth, and many countries had instituted policies to encourage people to remain in rural and less populated areas. Those administering the programmes needed information at the district and community levels. In Kenya, for example, each district had a Women's Development Committee, two members of which also served on the District Development Committee. They needed information on women at the district level;

(b) Where international migration was important, it might be useful to tabulate the labour force by migrant/non-migrant status. An example of that approach was given during the discussion by Francis Hloaele (Lesotho). In that country, women in the labour force were tabulated as follows:

Total number of women in the labour force:

(a) Currently working:

   (i) In Lesotho;

   (ii) Outside Lesotho;

(b) Job seekers:

   (i) Residents;

   (ii) Returned migrants;

and so on;

(c) Producers of statistics should bear in mind that indicators could sometimes be misleading. Users did not know how reliable a given indicator was, nor which indicators were best for making comparisons. It was up to producers of statistics to specify their limitations and to explain the concepts underlying the statistics;

(d) The line between producers and users was often blurred. Many agencies collected data in their own spheres of activity; others received data tabulations from the central statistical office. In either case, when agency personnel computed proportions and other statistics from those data, they were producing their own indicators. They might need help from the central statistical office in doing that or special short-term training in statistics;

(e) Was the framework presented earlier applicable to the situation in rural areas? Perhaps many of the indicators suggested in that paper were based on essentially modern or urban sector concepts. Indicators which were more relevant to the rural population should be developed.

3. Household composition, families and fertility

The Technical Co-ordinator introduced the discussion of statistics and indicators describing household composition, families and fertility. She began the consideration of those topics by pointing out that the family had been and still was the fundamental institution and organizational basis of African society and that most families lived in households. Thus, marital status and position in the family and household remained critical variables in determining a woman's social status and her access to resources.

She noted that there was wide variation across the region in the definition of a household as there were differences in the structure of households. Each country should develop a specific definition for statistical purposes appropriate to its own situation and then should make that definition very clear to users of statistics within and outside the country. Although most women in Africa were married and lived in households with male heads, an increasing number of women in the region were themselves heads of households. Some had never married and others were separated, widowed or divorced. Still others, because of extensive male labour migration or polygamy, were _de facto_ heads. As in the rest of the world, they were often the poorest, most disadvantaged households. Data on female heads had been unreliable because both survey interviewers and respondents tended to assign headship to any available male. However, special studies in the United Republic of Tanzania and Zambia suggested that female-headed households might constitute upwards of 20 per cent of all households.

The Co-ordinator pointed out that age at marriage was an important indicator of the situation of women because of its close association with fertility and age of childbearing. Available data made it clear that both mothers and babies were at greatest risk of death when the mother was very young (less than age 20), or relatively old (age 35 and over), or when pregnancies were too closely spaced (less than 2 years apart) or when the mother had had many births (five or more). By increasing the length of time a woman was at risk of pregnancy, early marriage increased her chances of bearing children before she had reached her twentieth birthday and of producing five or more children, thereby increasing the risks of mortality to herself and the children she would bear.

Although family sizes were somewhat lower in urban than in rural areas, particularly among educated women, African women and men continued to value high fertility. Crude annual birth rates were generally between 40 and 50 per 1,000 population and African women averaged a total of six to eight births. Because of very high infant and young child mortality rates, however, family sizes were somewhat lower than the fertility rate implied. About one in three children died before their fifth birthday and African families averaged approximately four surviving children. Educated women were more likely to achieve their desired family size through somewhat lower fertility and considerably lower infant and child mortality, but the differences in family sizes were not large.

The age pattern of fertility, however, was shifting during development as African women remained in school longer, took employment before marriage and married later. Accordingly, as development proceeded, the proportion of a women's lifetime fertility occurring before age 25 was decreasing. Moreover, as child survival rates improved and the knowledge and practice of modern methods of child-spacing spread, the percentage of lifetime fertility occurring at ages 35 and over also was decreasing. Relatively more women were able to achieve their desired family size by concentrating their fertility within the optimal childbearing ages - a development which itself contributed to improved child survival rates and reduced maternal mortality.

The Co-ordinator listed a number of important indicators of the situation of women in the family and household. Each of the indicators should be obtained separately for rural and urban areas where feasible:

(a) Households:

 (i) Average household size;

 (ii) Percentage of households with children under age 5 and age 15;

 (iii) Percentage with a female head;

 (iv) Percentage with absent male head;

(b) Nuptiality:

 (i) Legal age of marriage for women and men (where legal age of marriage for women was older than customary practice, it might be difficult to obtain accurate data on ages of married women);

 (ii) Percentage distribution of women and men by current marital status;

 (iii) Ages by which 50 per cent of women and 50 per cent of men had ever been married;

 (iv) Average difference in age between wives and husbands (that suggests the likelihood of a woman's becoming a widow);

 (v) Percentage of women in polygamous unions;

(c) Fertility:

    (i) Crude birth rate (CBR) - number of births in a given year divided by the estimated mid-year population (x 1000);

    (ii) General fertility rate (GFR) - number of births in a given year divided by the estimated mid-year population of women aged 15-49 (x 1000);

    (iii) Age-specific fertility rates (ASFR) - number of births in a given year to women of a given age group, divided by the mid-year number of women of that age group (x 1000);

    (iv) Total fertility rate (TFR) - the sum of age-specific fertility rates, used to approximate the total number of births a woman might be expected to have if she followed the age pattern of fertility existing at a given year;

    (v) Gross reproduction rate (GRR) - similar to TFR but computed on the basis of female births alone, that is, the average number of daughters per woman;

    (vi) Net reproduction rate (NRR) - GRR adjusted by female mortality rates from birth to the average age of childbearing. The NRR was therefore an indicator of the average number of daughters who were likely to survive to childbearing age. The difference between GRR and NRR was due to the level of female mortality in that society. Thus when multiplied by two, the NRR could be taken as an approximate indicator of surviving family size.

    (vii) Percentage distribution of lifetime fertility by age:

        a. Percentage under age 20;

        b. Percentage aged 20-34;

        c. Percentage aged 35 and over;

    (viii) Mean age at childbearing - the number of births in a given year weighted by the age of the women giving birth, summed, and divided by the total number of births.

The discussant for the topic was Gwen Lesetedi (Botswana), who presented some results of the 1981 census in her country. Questions on fertility were asked of all women aged 12-49. Between 1971 and 1981, fertility appeared to have risen somewhat - in 1971 the CBR had been estimated at 44.5 per 1,000 while in 1981 it had been estimated at 47.2. Differences in the age pattern of fertility were observed. Most of the births were to women aged 20-29. However, in 1981 the total fertility of women aged 45-49 averaged 6.4 births. Fertility was lower in urban than in rural areas, and declined with increasing education. Many births occurred outside of marriage - more than 50 per cent of births to women under age 30 were among the unmarried. A household in the 1981 census had been defined as those cooking together and living under the same roof. Because of high labour mobility to South Africa, 45.2 per cent of the urban households were headed by women and rates of female headship were still higher in the rural areas, where 83 per cent of the population resided. Household size averaged 4.3 persons in the cities and 5.8 in the country.

The points made in subsequent discussion focused on three issues: (a) improved communication and co-operation among producers and users of statistics; (b) usefulness of statistics and indicators compiled from existing data series; and (c) comments on specific demographic indicators.

On the issue of improved communication and co-operation the following points were made:

(a) Producers of statistics should also indicate their limitations;

(b) It was not enough for producers to note data limitations. The need for improved accuracy and reliability had to be addressed by pressing for improved resource allocation and policies to build a more effective statistical service;

(c) Users sometimes requested information without knowing how they would use it - or how to use it. Better dialogue between producers and users was essential, as was training for users;

(d) Many users were undertaking their own surveys and asking for help after the fact. Central statistical offices should be prepared to assist users define what they needed to know before they undertook their own surveys. The Mauritian Statistical Office, for example, was now working with the ministries to place a statistician at least part-time within each ministry.

On the issue of usefulness of indicators from existing statistical series the following points were made:

(a) The first priority was to make what women do visible. It was important therefore for users to work with producers to obtain gender-based tabulations of existing statistical series;

(b) Indicators must be selected to help answer questions and solve problems. The central statistical office and vital registration system could provide baseline population information, for example, but to understand the reasons for some phenomena, such as high fertility, and to develop policy, it was necessary to do additional research;

(c) Asking the right questions was the first step to solving problems. When a problem was understood, it was possible to define what information was needed and see what was already available. The focus should be on the problem, not on how much could be squeezed out of existing data;

(d) Statistics could reveal improvements as well as problems. Time series data were important in monitoring progress and in evaluating policies and programmes;

(e) Some types of action did not require large amounts of data. Policy decisions could be taken from knowledge gleaned from field workers and other sources.

On specific demographic indicators, the following points were made:

(a) The term "dependency burden" might be misleading, as some children worked while some adults were dependent. It was merely an indicator of age structure, not "dependency" per se;

(b) The problems of urbanization in developing countries were those of poverty, not merely the increasing number of people in cities. Dispersal of urban poverty back to the rural areas did not end poverty;

(c) Teen-age pregnancies were increasingly associated with social change during development as old constraints crumbled. It was important to monitor changes in age-specific fertility.

At the next session following the discussion, participants broke into four small working groups to begin the initial set of exercises on calculating, presenting and interpreting statistics and indicators relevant to women and development. The first set of exercises (see the "Exercises" section of the present report) dealt with population structure and change, geographical mobility and urbanization, marital status, household size and composition and the age structure of fertility. During that working session and those held over the next several days, demonstrations were also provided to each of the working groups on the calculation and presentation of statistics and indicators from the women's data base, Statistical Office of the United Nations, using a micro-computer and a spreadsheet programme.

C. Education, training and literacy

The third day of the seminar was devoted to a discussion of indicators of women's access to education, training and literacy. Topics discussed included school enrolment and achievement, curricula, vocational/technical training, literacy and adult education. Each topic was again introduced by one of the resource staff, followed by comments from one or more discussants and then a general discussion. During the final 90 minutes of the day, smaller groups were convened to work on exercises in compiling and interpreting educational statistics.

1. School enrolment and achievement

Mr. Makannah (Economic Commission for Africa) introduced the discussion of school enrolment and achievement by pointing out that the field of social statistics had actually begun with indicators of education. Those indicators were intended to give an overall picture of the state of education in the country. From there it was possible to measure the extent to which various sectors of the population had access to education and, to some extent, the quality of education.

Most regular educational systems were divided into the following levels: primary education, usually for children aged 6-11; secondary, usually for those aged 12-17; and post-secondary certificate, diploma or degree programmes. The situation of the regular educational system in a country could be described by the following measures:

(a) Crude enrolment ratio (CER) - total full-time enrolment at all three levels per 100 population, that is, the percentage of the total population enrolled in regular educational programmes;

(b) Gross enrolment ratio (GER) - total full-time enrolment at a given level divided by the estimated population eligible for that level. That was a refinement of the crude ratio, limiting both numerator and denominator at each level. The denominator for a given grade level was taken to be the total number of persons within the age range "normally" found at that level. Thus the primary level GER was calculated by dividing the number of primary school pupils by the total number of persons 6-11 years old, where 6-11 was the usual age of enrolment. That was a ratio, not a percentage, because primary school pupils might in fact be either older or younger than the "normal" ages;

(c) Percentage of female enrolment - the percentage of those enrolled at a given level who were female.

Mr. Makannah illustrated these indicators with figures from the 1982 UNESCO <u>Statistical Yearbook</u> for several of the countries represented at the seminar (see table 1). Those countries demonstrated considerable variation in enrolment ratios. Botswana, Lesotho and the United Republic of Tanzania were among those with primary GERs close to the UNESCO standard, that is, between 80 and 100, while others had GERs ranging between 40 and 60. Secondary GERs were much lower, from 3 per 100 to a maximum of only 23 per 100, against a standard of 60. Countries varied also in the percentage of enrolment that was female. At the primary level, females exceeded 50 per cent in the United Republic of Tanzania but made up only between 20 and 40 per cent in the other countries reviewed. At the secondary level, percentage of female enrolment dropped sharply from the first level overall and from year to year within the secondary level.

Table 1. Selected enrolment indicators

Country, level and year	Age group	Gross enrolment ratio (100)	Percentage female
Botswana			
Primary	6-12		
1975		80	55
Secondary	13-18		
1980		22	
1981		23	52
Ethiopia			
Primary	7-12		
1976		24	
1980		43	22
1981		46	
Secondary	13-18		
1975		6	
1980		11	36
1981		12	35
Post-secondary			
1981	13		
1982	13		
Malawi			
Primary	6-10		
1975		56	40
1980		59	41
Secondary	14-17		
1975		4	27
1980		4	29
1981		4	

The discussant for the topic was Abaynesh Makonnen (Ethiopia). She reporte that Ethiopia had had difficulty in obtaining reliable information until recently. In 1980 they had initiated an ongoing National Household Survey Programme, and they had recently completed their first population and housing census. They expected that denominators for rates would be much more reliable in the future. The Central Statistical Office had also had problems in obtaining reliable numerators from administrative records. The figures were not always properly compiled by the ministries and the Office did not have the necessary status and power to require improvements. Data were not compiled separately for rural and urban areas and data on drop-outs and on enrolment in vocational/technical programmes were not compiled.

The data they had, however, showed that female enrolment in grades 1-12 in 1981/82 constituted 35.1 per cent of the total. That represented some progress since 1974, when the comparable figure had been 31.5 per cent. The proportion of women with higher skills and of women in the professions was also low. A. Makonnen attributed low rates of school attendance to early marriage, pointing out that 53 per cent of the women aged 15-19 and a full 84 per cent of those aged 20-24 were married. The Central Statistical Office was looking to the Seminar to help them identify what was needed and which strategies could help them obtain the data.

In the discussion the following points were made:

(a) There was a serious problem with GER because the numerator and denominator did not refer to the same populations. Increases in GER might only indicate that there were a number of repeaters. As there was no way to solve this problem since it was inherent in the measure, users had to be aware of its limitations;

(b) If women were to have greater access to education, policies had to address traditional attitudes towards early marriage for women;

(c) Where teenage pregnancies were high, many girls dropped out of school and did not return after giving birth;

(d) Some countries did not have a policy of universal secondary education, so places for women often were not available. In the science streams, places for women were particularly limited;

(e) Many schools and universities had limited residential facilities for girls and women.

2. Indicators of access to appropriate curricula

The Technical Co-ordinator resumed presentation of issues on women's access to education, pointing out that one year of school completed at a given grade level, or one non-formal course attended by women and men, might not represent the same educational experience. Programmes offered to women and men were often very different in content and orientation and were frequently taught by teachers with different levels of experience and qualification. To understand the full pattern of educational opportunities, it was also necessary, therefore, to look at the kinds of institutions, programmes and curricula available to or taken advantage of by each sex.

The Co-ordinator noted that in much of the region, single-sex secondary and post-secondary institutions were the norm, and scientific and technical subjects were often found only in educational institutions or programmes for boys and men. She gave the following illustrations from 1973-1978 data for Kenya:

(a) Despite the fact that 80-90 per cent of women in rural areas were engaged in producing, processing or marketing food, access to technical education in agriculture was very limited. In 1973 at the Bankura Institute of Agriculture, there had been only 30 places for girls, compared to 270 for boys;

(b) In 1976, of the approximately 4,300 secondary school places, 30 per cent had been for girls. However, girls had been offered only 17 per cent of the places in science programmes;

(c) In 1978 no secondary vocational-technical schools had admitted women;

(d) Also in 1978, of the 21 secondary schools offering advanced mathematics, 15 schools had been for boys but only three for girls, while another three were co-educational.

Because Kenya had had a well-functioning Central Statistical Office for some time, such data were more readily available for that country, but the picture was much the same in most countries in the region.

Data from the Sudan for 1974 provided another example. Of the 974 secondary schools, the following distribution by type of secondary school and sex was reported:

	Number of schools		
	Female	Male	Total
General	250	609	859
Academic, higher	32	67	99
Commercial	0	3	3
Technical	0	11	11
Agricultural	0	2	2
Total	282	692	974

Even when technical programmes were offered to girls and women, the proportion electing to enrol was small. In part, that was the result of the absence of strong science and mathematics programmes for girls in the lower grades. Kenya had found it difficult to fill all the places available to girls in science, especially in physics. In Chad and Togo, few girls entered vocational-technical schools because few met the minimum entrance requirements. And among those enrolling in such schools, few girls graduated equipped with the kind of technical skills needed for modern rural development or with a foundation in math and science that was adequate for higher technical training. Some illustrations were given:

(a) In Lesotho, 58 per cent of those enrolled in vocational-technical schools in 1979 had been girls, but most studied domestic arts, bookkeeping and typing;

(b) In the Sudan, 16 per cent of those enrolled in higher specialized institutes in 1973/74 had been girls. They had constituted only 8 per cent of those enrolled in agriculture, business, engineering and architecture, combined, but 74 per cent of those enrolled in nursing, secretarial studies and teaching.

The same pattern usually was found at the university level. In Ghana in the mid-1970s, women had constituted only 7 per cent of the enrolment at the University of Science and Technology at Kumasi, and 20 per cent of those had been enrolled in the Faculty of Arts. Of the remainder, many had been in teacher training. In contrast, at the universities at Legon and Cape Coast, women constituted 15 per cent of the total enrolment, approximately twice their share of enrolment at Kumasi. Nevertheless, access to university training could permit a greater range of opportunity if women were ready to take advantage of it. Again in the Sudan, at the University of Khartoum, women were enrolled in the combined science faculties (agriculture, engineering, medicine, science, verterinary sciences, pharmacy) approximately in proportion to their total enrolment. Although their share of total enrolment was only about 10 per cent, fully 8.5 per cent of the science places were filled by women.

It was pointed out that efforts in recent years to make curricula more relevant to the vocational needs of African students might introduce even greater gender differentiation. For example, in the mid-1970s Ghana had introduced a new junior secondary school curriculum. It had offered home science and pre-nursing to girls, with electives in beauty culture, tailoring, dressmaking and catering. Boys had been offered an agricultural sciences programme, with electives in woodworking, masonry, technical drawing and automotive practice. Were such programmes to reflect the traditional African labour pattern in practice, most women would have been offered agricultural and business courses.

Data on enrolment by programme content and sex came from administration records. Three different types of statistics were useful, along with female/male ratios and percentage change over time for each:

(a) Enrolment rates in programmes of different kinds by sex. It was noted, however, that it was often difficult to select an appropriate denominator for those rates;

(b) Percentage distribution of enrolment in programmes of different kinds, by sex;

(c) Number of programmes of different kinds available to each sex.

The discussant for the topic was Samson D. Gumbo (Zimbabwe), who stressed the importance of developing curricula relevant to the real needs of rural women. Current curricula had been imported from developed western countries by those who themselves had been trained by a western-oriented educational system. Most parents saw a relevant curriculum as one leading to a white-collar job in an urban area, and despite their rhetoric about education for development, few politicians and educators would not select a classical western education for their children. Yet for the majority, such a curriculum resulted in education for unemployment and frustration. Upon leaving school, most were not equipped for urban white-collar jobs and few such jobs were available. Increasingly, the rural areas were seen as the province of unemployed men and of women and children.

However, to develop curricula relevant to rural development for both women and men, it would be necessary to address problems of both skills and attitudes. Before independence few women had enrolled in courses meant for men, but now a number of women were going into agriculture. Nevertheless, current technical curricula had been conceived as technical education for men, with content and components designed for men. It was not being fair to women to simply ask them to join in the same curriculum. Enrolment statistics should be used to monitor the participation of women and men in technical-vocational programmes, but that would not provide information about the relevance of those programmes to women's participation in rural development.

During the discussion, current efforts to re-orient educational curricula to encourage girls to study math, science and technical subjects in Ethiopia, Kenya, Malawi, the United Republic of Tanzania, Zambia and Zimbabwe were discussed. The following points were also raised:

(a) Educational statistics could not be considered in isolation from the development context. The national development strategy chosen and the educational system had to work in combination;

(b) Education for women was both a health and a development issue. The more education a woman had the higher were the chances of survival for her children and the better they did in school;

(c) In an attempt to make education for women relevant to their felt needs, it was important not to create separate programmes which marginalized women, channeling them away from training in key development skills;

(d) To increase the proportion of girls and women entering scientific and technical fields, it was necessary to start at any early age, in the home and in primary schools, to change expectations and develop skills;

(e) Career counseling was critically important in opening new fields to women;

(f) Career schemes still required western academic credentials. When jobs were advertised, employers looked upon graduates of technical schools as unqualified. The Government had to take the lead here;

(g) It was important to remember that indicators themselves did not suggest interventions. They were needed for monitoring and for evaluating the impact of policies and programmes. Although a single indicator might be inadequate to measure everything about education, it could be a place to begin. Improvement in the adequacy of educational indicators was a function of close dialogue between producers and users.

3. Indicators of literacy and adult education

Mr. Makannah (Economic Commission for Africa) introduced the discussion of literacy by reminding participants of the international definition: a literate person was one who could with understanding read and write a simple sentence on everyday life. Economists considered literacy one of the best indicators of socio-economic development. Common indicators on literacy included:

(a) Percentage of the population above a given age who were literate. Age 15 was most commonly used as the minimum age;

(b) Age-specific literacy rates;

(c) Female/male ratios of percentage literate.

The range of literacy in the region was wide. Some illustrative statistics were presented, as follows:

Country	Year	Age group	Percentage literate Total	Female	Male	F/M ratio
United Republic of Tanzania	1978	15+	78	70	78	0.90
Ethiopia a/	1980	10+	35	Not available		
Somalia	1980	15+	6	3	11	0.27
Zimbabwe	1980	15+	69	61	77	0.79

a/ Data subject to revision as a result of the recent census.

The Technical Co-ordinator then turned to the subject of women's access to adult education, that is, education outside the regular education programme, a topic closely related to literacy, as one often served as a vehicle for the other. She noted that, given low enrolment rates, developing countries faced a large and growing problem of out-of-school youth and young adults inadequately trained for employment in agriculture, business, industry and government, who swelled the ranks of the unemployed and underemployed. Those young people required vocational training. Most Governments and many non-governmental organizations had instituted programmes of vocational training for school leavers and extension services in rural areas. Consequently, the availability and content of such programmes provided another important set of indicators of women's access to education.

Data describing those courses came from administrative records and were often fragmentary because those courses were established under many different auspices, many of them ad hoc and ephemeral. Certain regularities had emerged from a series of ECA and World Bank case studies, however. Programmes for women generally were of two types. The first, often combined with literacy programmes, focused on homemaking, nutrition and health. While valuable, they rarely led to gainful employment. The second included such topics as hairdressing, dressmaking and the less skilled commercial subjects. While they did result in increased employability and earning capacity, the occupations were marginal. They did not help women qualify for participation in modern agriculture or achieve self-sufficiency and decreasing dependency. Courses for men focused on farm management and industrial innovation. There was an additional problem emerging as more employers were offering on-the-job training or apprenticeship programmes. Women could not qualify for those programmes unless they already had acquired the minimum skills necessary to get the job in the first place and qualify for advancement.

The Co-ordinator mentioned several useful indicators of access to out-of-school vocational and technical programmes that included:

(a) Number of courses offered, by type and sex of participants;

(b) Number and percentage distribution of those attending, by type of course and sex of participants;

(c) Female/male ratios of the above.

The discussant on the subjects of literacy and out-of-school education was Elizabeth Minde (United Republic of Tanzania). She stressed the importance of programmes which taught specific knowledge and skills as well as literacy. She noted that statistics on relative female and male literacy and access to training programmes could not get at the reasons behind the patterns observed. For example, very often residential facilities for women were not available at training centres.

During the discussion, efforts under way to improve women's access to literacy, education and training programmes in Botswana, Ethiopia, Kenya, Malawi, Zambia and Zimbabwe were described by participants from those countries and a number of problems pointed out. On women's access to training, the points raised included the following:

(a) Literacy, education and training were human rights and indicators of the extent of development of any society;

(b) Literacy:

   (i) Countries needed to know how many were illiterate, who they were, where they were distributed, how successful literacy programmes were, who was taking advantage of them, and so on;

   (ii) Data were needed on the application of literacy skills: how many school drop-outs were still literate? How many of those trained through literacy programmes lapsed into illiteracy through lack of ongoing opportunities to use their skills?

(c) Regular education:

   (i) Drop-off in enrolment ratios by grade might be the result of the absence of facilities, not lack of interest. Statistics were needed on the number of places, as well as on enrolment;

   (ii) Enrolment figures were affected by seasonal factors. That had to be accounted for in data collection;

(d) Vocational-technical programmes:

   (i) Data were needed to improve knowledge of women's access to relevant vocational and technical training, so that informed intervention was possible;

   (ii) Unless education and training were geared towards science and technology, research indicated that later job opportunities were unavailable except at the lowest levels;

   (iii) Men often assumed that women could not be away from home to participate in out-of-school courses. There was a need to educate men on that point;

   (iv) In countries where the Government was the main employer and certificates or other credentials were required, out-of-school training might not lead to employment or advancement. That led to frustration as there was no economic return from the new skills. The Government itself had to resolve that problem.

On the issue of collaboration between central statistical offices and administrative departments, the following points were made:

(a) Because central statistical offices generally had evolved from colonial structures, they had been dominated by men who often had a narrowly mathematical and statistical viewpoint. Wider participation in designing data collection activities was needed;

(b) Simple statistical skills could be taught in primary and secondary schools to broaden the ability of administrative officers to understand and interpret statistics and indicators;

(c) Establishment of small units which were outposts of the central statistical office in the different ministries was a useful way of improving administrative records and of co-ordinating research. Monthly meetings of the staff of such units with central statistical office staff helped to co-ordinate their efforts. Since many ministries offered their own training courses, it should be possible to compile information on those courses through such meetings;

(d) The administrative departments themselves had to improve their data. Ways must be found to facilitate the collaboration of the central statistical office and the administrative departments in improving administrative records and in highlighting women's access to them.

Participants emphasized that it was critically important that the Conference of African Planners, Statisticians and Demographers be made aware of the need for information on women in central statistical office and administrative departmental data collection activities.

D. Economic activity

On the fourth day of the seminar, participants considered a variety of indicators of women's economic activity - labour force participation, employment in formal and informal sectors, occupation, time use and access to credit and other economic resources and services. Special attention was given to the opportunities and needs of women in rural areas. Although the general schedule followed that of the previous days, two panel discussions were also held, with panelists drawn from participants, observers and resource staff.

1. Concepts and definitions

The Technical Co-ordinator introduced the day's topic with a review of currently accepted concepts and definitions of economic activity. She noted that development economists had recently come to recognize that improvement in the productivity of Africa's small farmers and businesses was critical for the region's development. As those were the very sectors in which women's economic activities were concentrated, programmes designed to improve the productivity of the small farmer and trader might be targeted inappropriately or have unexpectedly negative consequences if they were not based on adequate information about women's activities.

She noted that data on the labour force came from national censuses, special manpower surveys carried out on a household or enterprise basis and surveys taken for other purposes, such as the World Fertility Survey, which also asked about employment and occupation. However, it was now recognized that existing statistical systems using the labour force concept of economic activity had failed fully to represent the extent of women's productive role in African society. The shortcomings of existing data on the female labour force arose from a number of factors, some of which had already been mentioned, and those would be discussed more fully by later speakers. Three of the most significant factors were:

(a) A definition of the labour force which, derived from Western experience, was based on culturally biased assumptions about the sexual division of labour and economic relationships within the household;

(b) The practical difficulties of measuring part-time and multiple activities and production for own use as well as for exchange, particularly in the household setting;

(c) The costs for tabulation by sex of existing statistical series and for the collection of additional data.

Although different concepts and definitions of the economically active and greater sensitivity to sex biases in data collection and presentation were needed, the Technical Co-ordinator maintained that better exploitation of data from existing systems could highlight women's activities while identifying data gaps and conceptual inadequacies.

The Co-ordinator then traced the history and evolution of the concept of the labour force and its measurement from the 1920s, when the First and Second International Conferences of Labour Statisticians (ICLS) adopted the first set of international recommendations in that field. Since that time there had been a number of modifications in the definition of labour force participation and in the terminology to be employed in data collection. Most of those had been designed to facilitate differentiation among the employed, the underemployed and the unemployed. However, the most recent modification, at the 1982 meeting of the ICLS, called for the inclusion in the labour force - whether as an employee, unpaid family worker, or as self-employed - of anyone who could satisfy the requirement of a minimum of one hour's productive work during the reference week. She observed that the definition had to be very carefully applied if distinctions among the employed, underemployed and unemployed were not again to be obscured.

Participants were urged to read the seminar background documents (these are listed in annex VI to the present document) for a more thorough presentation of issues associated with statistics and indicators of women's economic participation. Important concepts and definitions discussed and illustrated there included:

(a) Activity status;

(i) Economically active (i.e., in the labour force);

a. Employed (i.e., currently working);

b. Unemployed (i.e., not currently working but looking or available for work);

     (ii) Not economically active;

(b) Status in employment;

     (i) Employer;

     (ii) Own-account worker;

     (iii) Employee;

     (iv) Unpaid family worker;

     (v) Member of producers' co-operative;

(c) Occupation;

(d) Industry (branch of economic activity);

(e) Sector of employment.

Useful indicators of women's labour force participation included:

(a) Number and percentage economically active, by sex;

(b) Female/male ratio of percentage economically active;

(c) Female share of the labour force (i.e. percentage female);

(d) Age-specific participation rates;

(e) Distribution by status in employment;

(f) Distribution by occupation;

(g) Occupational segregation;

(h) Distribution by industry;

(i) Segregation by industry;

(j) Rural and urban differentials in economic activity measures.

    Finally, she noted that some observers had suggested using a "partial activity rate" to monitor women's participation in the modern wage economy. That was defined as the percentage of women of particular age groups employed in certain specified modern occupational categories. However, that measure required occupational and industry data which were rarely available in the region. Moreover, since that measure would exclude the majority of African women, its use would frustrate the policy objective of making women's labour statistically visible, which would strengthen their claim on the national resources they needed to improve productivity.

2. Labour force participation

Misrak Elias (Eastern and Southern Africa Management Institute) served as chairman of a panel on labour force participation, employment (in both formal and informal sectors) and occupation. Panelists included Grace Bediako (consultant to the United Nations Secretariat), Elsa Teferi (Ethiopia), Celestina Ssewankambo (Zambia), F. Chatsalira (Malawi) and D. Ahawo (Kenya).

Ms. Elias gave a brief description of the Women in Development programme at the Eastern and Southern Africa Management Institute in the United Republic of Tanzania. Established in 1980 by ECA and supported by several international agencies, the programme was designed to train planners and managers in the region and sensitize them to women's contributions to economic development and to the impact of development programmes on women. The focus of the programme was on women but courses were offered to men as well as women. Among other topics, attention was given to methods of conducting research to clarify and measure women's economic activity.

Ms. Bediako, the first panelist, pointed out that occupational data by sex were needed to monitor changes in job segregation by sex. Since broad categories were not very useful for this, an occupational coding scheme at the greatest feasible level of detail was required. The United Nations publication distributed at the meeting, Compiling Social Indicators on the Situation of Women, gave the first two levels of the International Standard Classification of Occupations but more detailed breakdowns were useful. She illustrated the importance of the more detailed breakdowns by noting that although in one country women made up 43 per cent of all professional and technical workers, at a more detailed level they ranged from 1.4 per cent of airline pilots to 97 per cent of registered nurses, showing a high degree of occupational segregation at the detailed level.

Suggested indicators of occupational segregation included:

(a) Numbers by sex in various occupations, at as detailed a level as feasible;

(b) Percentage distribution by occupation: females (males) in a given occupation as a percentage of all employed females (males);

(c) Female share of a given occupation: females (males) in a given occupation as a percentage of all employed females (males);

(d) A segregation index of occupational distributions: sum of the differences between the percentages of male and female labour force in each occupation divided by 2. That indicated the percentage of men or women who would need to change jobs to equalize the occupational distribution.

Those indicators told whether women were disproportionately found in certain occupational sectors but they did not explain the distributions. Some of the differences observed might be the result of differences in educational and training opportunities for girls and boys. Others might be due to gender bias in hiring and promotion. Still others might arise from the perceived incompatibility of certain occupations with women's family responsibilities. Research would be necessary to determine the specific factors responsible for specific observed patterns.

Turning to country experience, Ms. Teferi described some of the changes in women's economic activity in Ethiopia in recent years. Data on labour force participation came from two establishment surveys, one in 1970 and a second in 1981. They referred primarily to urban unemployment. Two major shifts during the period were evident: prior to the revolution, 81 per cent of employed women worked in the private sector, but by 1981, 91.5 per cent of working women were employed in the public sector. During that period there had also been a shift of women into agriculture. Table 2 illustrates shifts in occupation and industry between 1970 and 1981.

Table 2. Shifts in women's employment: percentage distribution of women by industry and occupation, Ethiopia, 1970 and 1981

Area of employment	1970	1981
Industry		
Services/manufacturing	86.5	51.0
Agriculture	1.3	20.8
Trade/transportation	11.8	19.5
Finance/insurance	-	4.2
Construction/electronics, etc.	0.1	2.5
Other	0.3	2.0
All employed women	100.0	100.0
Occupation		
Production	43.0	47.6
Service	36.5	16.0
Clerical	9.1	20.9
Professional	7.6	2.1
Management	1.9	1.1
Other	1.9	12.3
All employed women	100.0	100.0

Since 1970, establishment surveys had covered only those employing 50 or more workers, but most women worked in household and small-scale establishments employing two or three workers, so women's employment and occupations in the informal sector were not well documented. Ms. Teferi urged that additional efforts be made to collect data on small-scale activities through small surveys and improved administrative records.

Another panelist, Ms. Ssewankambo, reviewed data on female economic activity in Zambia. Data came from three sources: the 1980 population census, annual establishment surveys in June or December and a 1983 detailed manpower survey. According to the 1980 census, women constituted only 35.5 per cent of a total labour force of 1,767,300. Moreover the rural and urban distribution of the labour force differed by sex: 73 per cent of the female labour force resided in rural areas while 81 per cent of the male labour force resided in urban areas (see table 3).

Data from annual establishment surveys showed that most women were employed in community, social and personal services occupations and in the traditionally female professions of teaching and nursing. Between 1975 and 1980, however, the number of women employed in agriculture and forestry doubled, from 1,100 to 2,300. When occupational data from the 1983 manpower survey were analysed by sex, they showed that females now were in many occupations which were previously male. She also noted that there appeared to be little difference in earnings between women and men. She said that a disproportionate number of working women reported themselves as unmarried. It was possible that many of those were in fact married but reported themselves as single to reduce tax liabilities. Once again, that illustrated the need to go behind the statistics themselves for full understanding.

Mr. Chatsalira reported that although small, the number of women employed in the modern sector in Malawi was increasing. Most were employed in teaching, clerical, sales and service occupations. The number of professionals was very small. Quoting from a study by David Hirschmann, published by ECA, he reported that the great majority of women in 1981 worked in agriculture at all levels: owners, employers, managers and full-time or casual employees, as follows:

(a) 3.6 per cent full-time workers on own holdings, in subsistence and significant cash cropping;

(b) 85.0 per cent full-time workers on own holdings, in subsistence and marginal cash cropping;

(c) 1.0 per cent full-time workers at low wages on estate farms;

(d) 5.5 per cent seasonal and part-time workers on small or medium-sized farms;

(e) 4.9 per cent other.

A new government policy to encourage female access to agricultural credit had resulted in up to 28 per cent female participation in such programmes.

Table 3. Rural and urban distribution of labour force, each sex, Zambia, 1981

(Percentage)

	Women	Men	Total
Rural	73	19	38
Urban	27	81	62
Total	100	100	100

Mr. Ahawo described Kenya's extensive system of labour statistics. In addition to population census data and a manpower survey conducted in 1981-1982, Kenya carried out an annual survey of establishments employing 50 or more workers. They had also undertaken a survey of the informal sector. To facilitate analysis they had developed a national occupational classification system. Data from establishment surveys from 1975 to 1983 indicated only a modest increase in women's labour force participation during the period. Salaried female employment increased only from 16 to 18 per cent and unsalaried from 23 to 29 per cent during that period.

Mr. Ahawo also noted a number of problems with labour force data. First among those was the continuing issue of defining the economically active. By counting only those at work or actively looking for work, discouraged workers were omitted. Moreover, by confining the establishment survey to those employing 50 or more and to urban areas, most unpaid family workers as well as employees of small-scale industries were omitted. The quasi-legal character of much non-formal economic activity made it difficult to obtain accurate information. Finally, he noted the importance of changing perceptions as the economy underwent evolution. Many men were now in so-called female occupations and many women were entering formerly male occupations, in some cases constituting up to 40 per cent of workers in those occupations.

The discussion that followed the panel presentations focused on the need for better information about nomadic women, on women employed in agriculture and the informal sector and on the special problems and opportunities of women employed in the formal sector. Concepts requiring clarification or redefinition were considered and data and research needs identified, as follows:

(a) For nomadic women, there was virtually no information on their activities, needs and special problems. Research was urgently needed;

(b) For women in agriculture:

(i) There was often no association between the levels of income women received and their activities in agriculture, nor was there a necessary association between land ownership and farming activities. Men usually owned the land and often controlled the farm's income while the women actually farmed the land;

(ii) There was need for improved data collection on economic activities in rural areas. Information was needed on property ownership or other collateral and access to credit. Ways also needed to be developed to measure individual contributions to household production. Although expensive, periodic censuses of agriculture should be undertaken;

(c) For women in the informal sector:

(i) It was important to refine the concept of informal activity and to devote resources to its measurement. That concern was stressed by participants from many of the countries;

(ii) Informal activity played an important role in building skills and amassing capital to enter the formal sector. Linkages between the informal and formal sectors should be researched;

(iii) Obstacles to success in the informal sector included lack of credit, low skills, limited access to raw materials, inadequate assessment of the market and competition from the often more efficient formal sector;

(iv) An ILO study of the informal sector in Botswana found important gender differences. Men tended to engage in mechanical/technical activities with higher profit potential, while women worked largely in beer brewing and food service activities. Even when men undertook so-called women's activities, they tended to be more aggressive, to work longer hours, and to derive better incomes. Botswana was now investigating the possibility of special benefit programmes for "small-scale industries", those employing fewer than 10 workers;

(d) For women in the formal sector:

(i) Public sector employment provided equal wages to women and men, but frequently the opportunities for advancement were not equal. Detailed occupational breakdowns would help to monitor the situation, but indicators of female advancement on the job were also needed;

(ii) Many were not willing to accept the concept of jobs that were incompatible with women's family responsibilities. Information was needed on marital instability and the special needs of women engaging in non-traditionally female occupations;

(iii) It was important to remember that what was a "female" occupation was culturally defined; in Uganda women engaged in construction, in Ghana they do not;

(iv) Sex bias was often evident in the categorization of workers in a household enterprise. Where both husband and wife engaged in related economic activities (e.g. spinning by wife, weaving by husband), the man was categorized as an own-account worker and his wife was usually counted as an unpaid family worker. Using gender-free definitions, both would be counted as own-account workers;

(e) For data and research needs and methods (beyond those already mentioned):

(i) It might be difficult to operationalize the shift in definition of unpaid family workers who were economically active from those working at least one third time to those working one hour per week or more. It was not always easy to know when one is at work. The borderline between work and household chores or work and leisure activity was often ambiguous. Research was necessary to clarify and delimit economic activities under the new definition;

(ii) At what age did work begin? What about the work of children? It might be necessary to set subregional and national standards to supplement international recommendations. Perhaps two sets of some tables would need to be published: those incorporating local/national standards and those using subregional or international standards;

(iii) Results from specialized surveys could help develop new questions on economic activity for the more routine census and other data collection programmes. Essential dimensions might include:

   a. Type of principal, secondary, tertiary activities;

   b. Location of each activity;

   c. Whether full-time, part-time, casual;

   d. Length of time spent at each;

   e. Number of days worked last week;

   f. Status in employment: own-account, employer, manager, employee, member of producers' co-operative;

   g. Whether paid or unpaid (is a pay slip given?);

   h. Amount received;

(iv) Several producers of statistics indicated a new appreciation of how users could be of assistance:

   a. In designing questionnaires and other data collection instruments;

   b. In developing the tabulation programme;

(v) Producers also indicated that they would take more initiative in involving users as well, but they also expected their fellow participants from the user side to take the initiative in requesting the information they needed.

3. Time-use studies

The session concluded with a description by the representative of the Statistical Office of the United Nations Secretariat of data collection programmes for recording and analysing individuals' allocation of time. Known as time-budget or time-use studies, they charted out the pattern of activities during a 24-hour day, usually at different times of the year where seasonality was an important factor.

Three methods had been used:

(a) Observation, either continuously over a long period of time or at randomly designated times;

(b) Verbal recall of the events of the previous day;

(c) Records kept by subjects of their activities and the time spent in each.

The Seminar was informed that a number of small anthropological time-use studies had been carried out in Africa, but only three national-level studies had been undertaken in the region as they were difficult and costly. Botswana had had two and the Ivory Coast one such study. Nevertheless, they were extremely useful, as they covered aspects of behaviour not otherwise easily available. All activities were recorded. Selection and aggregation were left to the researcher for further analysis. The studies had two major uses: to learn about the range of activities in a pilot study in order to design a standard labour force survey, and to broaden a country's ability to measure its subsistence production and other productive activities not easily measured.

Some of the difficulties which must be noted and overcome in carrying out time-allocation studies were pointed out:

(a) The problem of selecting a typical day: In Botswana one study observed the subject once a month, on a randomly selected day, for a 12-month period. The second study made observations four times per year. In the Ivory Coast urban subjects were observed for one week once a year, rural subjects four times per year for one week;

(b) The coding scheme for such a wealth of data;

(c) The effect on the people being observed: With sufficient familiarity, this effect tends to wear off. Accordingly, one should build in extra observation days where feasible;

(d) Training of observers/interviewers and length of time of the interview;

(e) Subjects who did not go by clock time: Reference events - sunrise, noon, call to prayer, and so on - could be used.

Among other findings, the studies illuminated the economic costs and value of children to their parents and helped to explain differentials in school attendance. They also showed that women and girls tended to work longer hours than men and boys and highlighted the important roles women played in agriculture, animal husbandry and trade. Table 4 shows data from the 1979 Ivory Coast time allocation study illustrating the relative working hours of women and men.

Table 4. Contribution of women and men aged 15 and over to different sectors of economic activity, Ivory Coast, rural areas, first quarter 1979

	Activities	Average time per day (hours and minutes) Male	Female	Share of total work hours, each sex (percentage) Male	Female
1.	Market economic activities	2:31	1:25	61	39
2.	Subsistence economic activities	0:49	1:45	29	71
1+2	Total	3:20	3:10	48	52
3.	Domestic work	0:35	3:38	13	87
1+2+3	Productive work burden	3:56	6:48	34	66

4. Economic activity in rural areas

The next session was devoted to consideration of women's economic activity in rural areas. Mr. Kuezi-Nke (ECA/Zambia), chaired a panel of participants and observers. Panelists included D. Alonzo (Food and Agriculture Organization (FAO)), A. Makonnen (Ethiopia), H. Terefe (Ethiopia), R. Nkomo (Zimbabwe), C. Ssewankambo (Zambia), B. Madsen (United Nations Development Programme), G. Mulindi (Kenya).

The session opened with the presentation by the representative of FAO of portions of his paper on statistics and indicators on the role of women in agriculture and rural development. He presented a series of indicators which had been found to be useful in five key policy areas: labour force participation and economic activity; access to land, water and other natural resources; access to inputs, markets, agricultural information and services; people's participation; and access to education and training. (A full listing of suggested indicators is given in that paper.)

Indicators of rural labour force participation included:

(a) Women in agriculture as a percentage of the economically active female population;

(b) Percentage distribution by employment status (own-account worker, unpaid worker, agricultural employee, and so on) of women economically active in agriculture;

(c) Women as a percentage of landless agricultural workers;

(d) Percentage of landless rural households headed by women;

(e) Female as a percentage of male median weekly or monthly wage of agricultural labour, by type of work;

(f) Rural unemployment and underemployment by sex;

(g) Women agricultural traders as a percentage of all agricultural traders.

He noted that there were many problems in the standard concepts and that the development of an adequate set of indicators was a slow process, requiring dialogue between producers and users. It was particularly important that better approaches to village level statistics and to farm data be developed.

Ms. Makonnen and Ms. Terefe described efforts in Ethiopia to obtain data on the economic activities of the rural population. As part of the National Integrated Household Sample Survey Programme, the rural labour force was surveyed quarterly, using the farmers' associations as the primary sampling unit. A special module had also been developed for nomadic populations. In those surveys respondents were asked about both current (previous week) and usual (previous three months) activities. The same definitions were used in urban and rural areas. Because of enumerator bias and the defects in concepts and definitions already noted by others, thorough enumerator training and supervision were required. Enumerators must be trained to ask additional follow-up questions where appropriate. Ninety-six per cent of rural economically active women were in agriculture. Most economically active rural women were counted as unpaid family workers while men appeared as own-account workers. Since children were economically and socially useful to women, early marriage and high parity were encouraged.

Ms. Nkomo described the role of women in the resettlement programme which Zimbabwe had undertaken since independence. Since the programme began, 32,000 household heads had been resettled. Of those, 5 per cent were women, primarily divorced and widowed. If a woman qualified, she had access to a land permit and to credit, extension services and marketing services. Few women owned oxen. Because they must hire draught power, they usually had to wait until the animal's owner had finished, which tended to hold them back. These women usually settled near relatives for help.

She pointed out that it was important to make return visits to see how women were faring under the resettlement scheme. While the traditional sexual division of labour had not changed in the new settlements, a change in life-style had occurred - the land was economically more viable. The income target per household was $400 and it might go higher. She expected women's status to improve eventually. Relatively few women or men participated in non-agricultural activities. A major survey of the resettlement areas was expected to begin in June 1985.

Ms. Ssewankambo reported that in the agricultural provinces of Zambia, 14.5 per cent of the households were headed by women. Women and men generally grew different crops, with women focusing on food crops. Information on returns from crop sales by sex were unavailable. Credit was freely available to both women and men and many participated in co-operatives.

Ms. Madsen discussed the problem of rural women's access to credit. Most women did not have collateral, nor did they know how to go about approaching financial institutions for credit. One way to overcome the problem of collateral was to use the income-generating potential of a women's co-operative, not the individual household, as the basis for guaranteeing a loan. To make sure that women knew how to seek credit, a manual for rural extension agents could be useful. Zambia's co-operative credit scheme and its Agricultural Finance Company had earmarked funds for small-scale women farmers. The Village Industrial Service had a revolving fund to make loans to small-scale industries begun by female entrepreneurs.

Ms. Mulindi reported that in Kenya almost all women in the rural areas worked on their own family holdings and noted that this was true for only 20 per cent of the men. Most women were counted in labour force statistics as helpers, that is, unpaid family workers on their husband's farm.

In the discussion that followed, several references were made to the need for conceptual clarity and improved measurement of women's activities at rural and village levels. Several participants indicated progress in or plans for carrying out rural agricultural labour force surveys to gather the kinds of information recommended by Mr. Alonzo. Others re-emphasized the importance of squeezing more information out of existing data. It was pointed out by the participant from Lesotho that the effects on women of labour migration to South Africa were seen most dramatically in the rural areas. Accordingly, the Government had set up rural labour funds to assist women left behind.

Finally, participants were reminded once again of the need to get behind the statistics and indicators to understand what was really going on by an example offered by one participant. Since colonial days in her country, as in much of Africa, men had been responsible for cash cropping while women had traditionally grown the food for local consumption in fields reserved for that purpose. However, in one region, despite the fact that women had continued to provide much of the agricultural labour, Ministry of Agriculture statistics showed that production of maize, the key cash crop, had become increasingly important while production of food crops, particularly of ground-nuts, had declined steadily for more than 20 years. To find out what was happening to cropping patterns and to the traditional division of labour and income in the region, ministry staff had talked separately to women and men and found that as the price of maize increased, the men had taken over land traditionally used by women for food crops to expand maize production. Meanwhile, the decrease in land available for production of food crops, together with the additional time women were required to devote to the expanded maize fields, meant that the women were having to purchase food for their families at increasingly higher prices. But, since the men continued to control all income from the sale of cash crops, the extra cash from the additional maize production was not available to the women to buy that food, and nutritional status was showing some deterioration. Without that kind of detailed investigation, going behind the statistics, it would not have been possible to understand the true situation of women in that region, nor to begin to plan for effective intervention.

At the next session, participants reassembled in small groups to work on exercises to develop and interpret statistics and indicators of women's economic activity.

E. Health and health services

The morning session of the fifth day of the Seminar was devoted to a discussion of indicators of health. Once again, each of the subtopics was introduced by a member of the resource staff, followed by comments from participant discussants and general discussion. During the last 90 minutes of the morning session, participants returned to their working groups to carry out a series of exercises on health and health service statistics.

The Technical Co-ordinator began the consideration of health indicators by pointing out that the World Health Organization defined health as a state of complete physical, mental and social well-being, but because they did not know how to measure such an ideal state, health continued to be described in terms of the absence of disease, disability and premature death. The availability and accessibility of health services were described in terms of access to those persons and facilities that treated illnesses.

She noted that there were at least six major purposes for which women's health statistics and indicators were sought:

(a) To identify the special health problems and service needs of women;

(b) To plan service delivery programmes to meet those needs;

(c) To manage and deliver those services in a cost-effective manner;

(d) To monitor the absolute and relative availability, accessibility and coverage of health services for all women and particular subgroups;

(e) To monitor changes in health status and in access to services over time;

(f) To assess the impact of health services and specific programmes on the health of women.

Statistics and indicators were needed by a variety of health data users, each with different data needs, including policy makers, health and women's programme planners and managers, health service delivery personnel and their supervisors, donor agencies, outside evaluators and the like. The operating principle in developing a system of health status and health service indicators must be to ensure that information was available for decision-making where and when the decisions must be made. Although routine service statistics were the basic indicators for managing and monitoring service delivery, those must be supplemented for policy and programme development by information from other sources, such as censuses, civil registration systems, morbidity surveys and special studies.

1. Health status

Referring to table 5, the Co-ordinator pointed out that health status indicators were developed from statistics on births, deaths, disease and disability. Obtained from a variety of sources, the data were usually tabulated by

Table 5. Potential sources of data on health and health services

Statistical series	Population census	Household surveys	Focus groups	Registration systems	Administrative records (public works, health, insurance, education, etc.)
A. Health status					
1. Births:					
by maternal characteristics			Demographic		Birth registration
by characteristics of child (sex, birth weight, outcome)			Demographic		Service statistics
by characteristics of the delivery		Demographic			Service statistics
2. Deaths					
(a) Infant/child: by age, sex, cause		Demographic		Death registration	Service statistics
(b) Maternal: by age, parity, cause				Death registration	Service statistics
(c) Other: by age, sex, cause	two censuses			Death registration	Service statistics
3. Disease, disability: by age, sex, cause		Morbidity, nutrition, immunization (EPI)		Notifiable disease reporting system / Surveillance system (EPI)	Service statistics / Insurance claims
B. Health services					
1. Availability	Census for population base				Administrative records: Personnel, training Facilities Programmes Drugs, supplies, etc.

-46-

Table 5 (continued)

Statistical series	Population census	Household surveys	Focus groups	Registration systems	Administrative records (public works, health, insurance, education, etc.)
2. Accessibility: by sex, age, other characteristics	Census for population base: by small area	KAP [a] (health, family planning, nutrition)	KAP		Administrative records: As above, by location
3. Utilization/coverage: by age, sex, residence health problem/ reasons	Census for population base: by small area	Utilization consumption, (health, family planning)	KAP	Clinic registration, insurance enrolment, water/sewer hookups	Service statistics Insurance claims Water consumed Sewerage treated
4. Expenditures		Utilization, household expenditure			Records of receipts Insurance claims paid
5. Costs					Budgets Expenditure records
6. Effectiveness: Quality Health status Availability Utilization/ coverage	As above	As above	KAP	As above	As above
7. Cost/effectiveness	As above	As above		As above	As above

[a] KAP – Knowledge, attitude, practice.

-47-

age (or age of women giving birth), sex and rural and urban residence. Where feasible, those data were also tabulated by specific disease or cause of death and by a variety of socio-demographic characteristics, both of individuals and of households. She then turned to a detailed discussion of the three general categories of health status indicators: those associated with fertility, mortality and the incidence and prevalence of disease, that is, morbidity.

(a) <u>Fertility indicators</u>

A paradox existed in considering fertility statistics as indicators of women's health status. On the one hand there was a positive association between health and fertility, as women who were very ill were often unable to conceive or to bear a live child. On the other hand, women who had many or closely spaced births or who became pregnant at very young or very old reproductive ages tended to be at higher risk of mortality themselves, and so were their children. If that ambiguity was kept in mind, fertility statistics could be useful indicators of women's overall health situation.

(i) <u>Sources and problems</u>

Fertility data came from demographic surveys and from birth registration systems. In some cases indicators might be derived from service statistics, and in others they might be estimated from census data.

Under-reporting of both births and infant deaths, poor age reporting, poor coverage of vital registration systems and poor statistical coverage of births outside the health systems (the great majority) were common limitations of fertility data in most developing countries.

(ii) <u>Indicators</u>

The fertility indicators discussed in the previous session on population were crude birth rate, general fertility rate, total fertility rate, gross reproduction rate and net reproduction rate. Indicators of high-risk births were:

(a) Proportion of births to teenagers and to older women, that is, proportion of births to women under age 20 and over age 34;

(b) Proportion of high-parity births, that is, births of parity 5 and over;

(c) Proportion of births at less than 24 months after the previous birth;

(d) Proportion of low-weight births, that is, births of less than 2,500 grams (an indicator of prematurity);

(e) Proportion of births not attended by trained personnel.

An indicator of protection against high-risk pregnancy was the percentage using contraceptives, by method.

(b) Mortality indicators

The Co-ordinator began the discussion of mortality indicators by pointing out that death was not in itself a particular indicator of the prevalence of ill health. However, when relatively more people died at earlier ages in some populations than in others, when people died from particular causes which need not have resulted in death given proper preventive or curative care or when the expected sex differences in age-specific mortality narrowed or were reversed, then mortality statistics became indicators of health status.

She described the general age pattern of mortality by sex and age observed in all human populations, noting that although societies at different economic levels might show different levels of mortality, the general shape of the mortality curve by age was similar in all societies. It began high, fell off rapidly during pre-school years and remained low until the late teens when it gradually began to climb again, accelerating after the 40s and 50s to the point where eventually it reached 100 per cent.

The shape of the mortality curve was similar for women and men, but the sexes commonly differed in levels of mortality. Females were usually at a lower risk of death at all ages. Accordingly, a relatively high level of the mortality curve or any departure from the normal shape of that curve or a female curve that crossed the male curve, all signalled the presence of serious health problems in a population and called for investigation into the reasons why particular groups were at an abnormal risk of death. Alternatively, they might signal deficiencies in the mortality data available by sex and age.

(i) Sources and problems

Mortality data came from demographic surveys, civil registration systems, service statistics, verbal autopsies and censuses.

Under-reporting of deaths at all ages, but particularly of infants, under-reporting of female deaths at all ages, misrepresenting of ages, poor coverage by the registration system and unreliable cause-of-death data were major limitations of mortality data in most developing countries.

(ii) Indicators

Indicators of death (mortality) rates included:

a. Crude death rate (CDR): deaths per 1,000 mid-year population;

b. Infant mortality rate (IMR): deaths of children under 1 year per 1,000 births during that year;

c. Child mortality rate (CMR): deaths of children aged 1-4 per 1,000 births during previous 4 years;

d. Age-specific mortality rate (ASMR): deaths in a given age group per 1,000 total mid-year population of that age group;

      e. Relative female mortality:

          (i)   Female/male ratios of mortality rates;

          (ii) Female share of mortality: percentage of deaths at a given age that were female;

      f. Survival:

          (i)   Percentage of births who survived to age 5 (or conversely percentage of births who died before age 5), by sex;

          (ii) Female/male ratio of percentages who survived to age 5;

      g. Maternal mortality: Female deaths associated with childbearing per 1,000 women aged 15-49 (or female deaths at ages 15-49 per 1,000 women aged 15-49);

      h. Expectation of life at birth (or at some other age), by sex: average number of years left to live at birth (or at the reference age), given the currently prevailing sex and age-specific pattern of mortality. That was a summary measure of overall mortality pattern. It was useful but fairly complicated to calculate.

(c) *Morbidity indicators*

    The Co-ordinator briefly reviewed the differences between the pattern of diseases in industrialized countries and that in developing countries. Developing country populations carried a heavy burden of illnesses, many from causes that were once prevalent in the developing countries: communicable diseases, such as measles or polio, parasitic diseases, such as malaria or hookworm, diarrhoeal diseases often associated with sanitary practices and respiratory disease. She suggested that much of that disease burden was the result of poverty and the slow pace of economic development, noting that even in poor countries few of the elite suffered severely from such diseases. She also pointed out the special problem in developing countries of a synergism between infectious disease and malnutrition, each contributing to the other and often setting the young child under 5 on a downward spiral to chronic illness, undernutrition and even death. For that reason, indicators of nutritional status were of major importance in monitoring health. Moreover, since female undernutrition during pregnancy was a major cause of prematurity, which in turn was a major cause of infant death, female nutritional status was an important indicator of both women's health and that of their children.

    (i) <u>Sources and problems</u>

    Morbidity data came most commonly from service statistics. For certain particular diseases, they might also come from special registration systems, surveillance systems or reports of "notifiable" diseases, such as cholera. Morbidity or nutrition surveys, either stand-alone or as modules in other household survey programmes, occasionally provided very useful data. Where countries had systems of social insurance, data on insurance claims might provide morbidity data.

It was difficult to monitor morbidity levels in the population, as the numbers reported by most statistical services represented only those who had used health services or otherwise come to the attention of the authorities. Sources were also subject to limitations from under-reporting, age-misreporting, and the like.

(ii) Indicators

Useful indicators of morbidity included:

a. Diseases (total and by cause, by sex):

   (i) Incidence: number of events per 1,000 population, per year;

   (ii) Prevalence: number with specific condition per 1,000 population;

b. Disability (total and by cause, by sex):

   (i) Temporary: number of days lost from normal activity per year per person;

   (ii) Permanent: number of permanently disabled per 1,000 population;

c. Nutritional status:

   (i) Weight for age, by sex (up to 5 years of age);

   (ii) Proportion of under 5s below 80 per cent, 80-89 per cent, 90-99 per cent of standard weight for age;

   (iii) Weight for height, by sex;

   (iv) Proportion "wasted", i.e. below 80 per cent (severe), 80-89 per cent (moderate), 90-99 per cent (mild) of standard weight for height, by sex;

   (v) Height for age, by sex;

   (vi) Proportion "stunted", i.e. below 80 per cent (severe), 80-89 per cent (moderate), 90-99 per cent (mild) of standard height for age by sex;

   (vii) Proportion of women with nutritional anemia;

   (viii) Per capita consumption of calories, by sex;

   (ix) Proportion of population below norm for consumption of calories, by sex;

   (x) Proportion of population below norm for consumption of animal protein, by sex.

The discussant for this topic was Ms. I. P. Mafethe (Zimbabwe), who underscored the key role of nutrition in health. Despite a major effort in Zimbabwe to extend primary health services to the rural areas, the effect would be small unless adequate nutrition was provided in the home. In rural Zimbabwe as in most of Africa, it was women who were responsible for providing food for the family and who were therefore the key to good family nutrition. When resources were limited, women tried to ensure that the children were adequately fed, often by reducing their own intake to a minimum. Since they must continue to till the land and carry a heavy load of other work, their health suffered. To affect significant change in that situation, men as well as women must be taught the importance of good nutrition for women and children and must assume responsibility for nutrition in the decisions they made about the allocation of family resources.

2. Health services

Turning to indicators of health services, the Co-ordinator noted that for a number of reasons - including the high cost of the western model of medical care, the nature of common health problems, which were primarily either preventable or easily treated at home if the caretaker knew what to do, and cultural preferences for traditional healers and birth attendants - most of the countries in the region were experimenting with a multilevel health care system, combining western medicine with certain aspects of traditional care. At the apex of the health care pyramid was usually the university teaching hospital, with its super-specialties, research and training. It served as the specialty referral centre for the entire population. Below that were general or community hospitals and maternity hospitals, providing the next level of in-patient care and referral services for the community. At a still lower level of sophistication and serving a smaller area were the health centres and polyclinics. Geographically and medically more limited still were the local clinics, and finally at the base of the health system pyramid were the various kinds of village health posts and dispensaries. Virtually all African countries were now training new cadres of staff to work at the local clinic and village level and were training traditional birth attendants in safe methods of delivery and referral of difficult cases. Many were also encouraging health system staff to co-operate with traditional healers where appropriate and were investigating the use and effectiveness of traditional herbal remedies.

Referring again to table 5, the Co-ordinator indicated that however the particular national system was structured, there were six dimensions to be considered if countries were to develop appropriate policies and programmes for the effective and equitable provisions of health care to women and men: availability, accessibility (physical, financial, social/cultural), utilization (coverage achieved), quality, effectiveness and cost-effectiveness.

Indicators of availability came primarily from administrative records of the ministries of health and education, supplemented by population censuses and manpower surveys. Some common indicators were based on health personnel by type per 1,000 population, including:

(a) Midwives per 1,000 women 15 to 49 years;

(b) Nurses, physicians per 1,000 population;

(c) Hospitals beds, other facilities per 1,000 population.

Data on geographical accessibility came from administrative records for small areas plus the censuses for socio-cultural and financial accessibility. Data came from household utilization and KAP (knowledge, attitude, practice) surveys for indicators on health, nutrition and family planning.

Some useful indicators of accessibility included:

(a) Proportion of population in areas with inadequate availability of medical personnel (that is, less than average, less than some norm);

(b) Proportion of population in areas with an inadequate number of health facilities, including hospital beds;

(c) Proportion within X kilometres of the nearest health facility;

(d) Proportion with access to safe water;

(e) Proportion with access to sanitary waste disposal.

Data for indicators of utilization (coverage achieved) came from service statistics, utilization surveys, consumption and expenditure surveys and KAP surveys.

Some useful indicators included:

(a) Per capita number of visits to different types of practitioners or facilities, by sex and age;

(b) Percentage of population by sex and age visiting different types of practitioners or facilities;

(c) Percentage of deliveries attended by trained personnel;

(d) Percentage of deliveries in hospital, maternity or health centres;

(e) Percentage of eligible women using family planning;

(f) Percentage of children aged 5-14 immunized against specific diseases, by age and sex;

(g) Percentage of children fully immunized.

As the quality of health services was difficult to measure, the total per capita level of expenditure for health services overall or for a particular service for the entire population or for particular subgroups was often taken as a substitute.

Data came from administrative records or receipts, insurance claims paid and from household surveys of income and expenditure. Indicators included series on per capita expenditures for particular services by particular subgroups.

Effectiveness was measured by changes in indicators of health status and of health care availability, accessibility, coverage achieved and expenditure levels. They required time-series data from the sources mentioned above.

Sources for indicators of costs were administrative records, including budgets and agency expenditure records. In combination with the measures of effectiveness discussed above, indicators of cost-effectiveness could be developed showing cost per service, classified by effectiveness and by coverage achieved.

Discussants for this topic were S. E. Chikwana (Zimbabwe), I. P. Mafethe (Zimbabwe) and Cletus P. B. Mkai (United Republic of Tanzania).

Mr. Chikwana recounted the efforts made since independence in Zimbabwe to reduce the gross imbalance in health services between urban and rural populations and described some of the constraints and achievements in implementing that objective. Although many problems remained, significant progress had been made. Goals and achievements included:

(a) Improvement of availability and accessibility of health centres so that there was one health centre for every 5,000-10,000 population and within 8 kilometres or one-hour walking time of each household. To achieve that, a target had been set for the construction of 326 new health centres and the upgrading of existing clinics and centres within 5 years. To date, 210 new centres had been constructed, each staffed with two medical assistants and three aides;

(b) Free health care for families earning less than $Z 150 per year;

(c) More trained personnel, especially village health workers (VHWs);

(d) Access to safe water and sanitary waste disposal for all households;

(e) Full immunization for all children under 9 years of age. By 1982 24 per cent had been fully immunized;

(f) Adequate nutritional status for all children;

(g) Integrated maternal and child health services, including child-bearing.

Key indicators in 1982 were estimated as follows:

(a) Crude birth rate (CBR), 49 per 1,000;

(b) Crude death rate (CDR), 15 per 1,000;

(c) Infant mortality rate (IMR), 60 per 1,000;

(d) Maternal mortality, 130 per 100,000.

Continuing problems included the shortage of trained personnel, the reluctance of many health workers to accept postings in rural areas and an inadequate health information system for assessing needs and planning, monitoring and evaluating services. To address the latter, Zimbabwe had established a pilot health information system in 1984, now being tested in two districts.

Ms. Mafethe pointed out the importance of knowing about the availability of health workers at the district and community level if planning for services to the rural population was to be adequate. She illustrated the level of information needed with a table showing the distribution of village health workers at the district level in Zimbabwe (see table 6). From such data, targets could be set and progress towards the goals monitored.

Mr. Mkai discussed the usefulness of a household survey programme that contained a health module for generating morbidity and service utilization data. In the United Republic of Tanzania such a module yielded the following information:

(a) Proportion ill during the previous week:

(i) Approximately 9 per cent of both sexes;

(ii) By age (percentage of each age group):

Age	%
Less than 1 year	14
1-4	14
5-14	6
15-64	9
65+	22

(b) Distribution of illness by symptoms (percentage distribution):

Illness	%
Fever	28
Diarrhoea	16
Cough	6
Malaria	2
Measles	2
Colds	2
Other	44

Table 6. Distribution of village health workers, by district, Zimbabwe, 1985

District	Population	Families	Villages	Persons per village	Families per village	Village health workers Previous estimate	Village health workers Current estimate	Number trained
MANICALAND								
Buhera	168 000	32 762	204	809	161	418	408	98
Chimanimani	56 000	10 492	105	667	100	159	210	82
Chipinge	139 000	26 311	175	1 006	150	263	310	93
Kutare	129 000	21 262	169	994	126	250	250	93
Kutaza	92 000	22 612	162	796	140	183	225	96
Nyanga	70 000	17 076	154	584	603	174	198	82
Rusape	147 000	22 905	163	1 160	141	292	310	92
						1 739	1 911	636
MASHONALAND CENTRAL								
Bindura	29 000	6 579	58	672	112	56	65	
Centenary	15 000	4 787	53	566	90	75	75	
Concession	57 000	15 265	78	1 141	196	113	156	
Guruve	71 000	14 559	112	884	130	141	160	
Mt. Darwin	60 000	15 055	95	1 032	158	158	190	
Rushinga	47 000	8 316	83	964	100	157	138	
Shamva	36 000	7 602	69	740	110	71	75	
						771	859	
MASHONALAND EAST								
Goromonzi	57 000	8 461	60	1 100	141	114	114	93
Marondera	50 000	6 561	53	906	124	99	99	74
Mudzi	68 000	13 516	84	1 012	161	224	198	74
Murewa	109 000	23 771	138	1 022	172	217	276	79
U M P	63 000	14 354	90	944	159	175	180	75
Mutoko	71 000	12 723	114	947	112	178	158	81
Seke	29 000	4 902	48	979	102	57	57	67
Wedza	43 000	7 796	72	764	108	86	90	62
						1 150	1 172	605

Table 6 (continued)

District	Population	Families	Villages	Persons per village	Families per village	Village health workers Previous estimate	Village health workers Current estimate	Number trained
MASHONALAND WEST								
Chegutu	60 000	11 357	112	607	101	117	120	100
Chinhoyi	66 000	14 321	102	725	140	131	130	85
Kadoma	22 000	4 873	39	744	125	40	40	73
Ngezi	27 000	8 222	78	628	105	53	78	65
Kariba	10 000	1 409	26	538	54	50	60	45
Karoi	97 000	20 277	114	1 044	178	194	204	69
					539	585	596	437
MATEBELELAND NORTH								
Binga	47 000	10 532	97	856	109	188	188	76
Hwange	38 000	8 876	84	643	106	96	96	76
Inyathi	27 000	4 151	54	741	77	54	80	74
Lupane	63 000	12 442	130	887	96	156	136	83
Nkayi	87 000	14 858	151	940	98	217	210	83
Tsholotsho	86 000	10 349	114	1 079	91	214	214	85
						925	924	477
MATEBELELAND SOUTH								
Beitbridge	52 000	5 204	54	963	96	104	104	82
Gsigodini	37 000	6 291	59	1 017	107	167	98	96
Filabusi	44 000	6 237	61	869	102	87	88	58
Guanda	84 000	12 196	103	951	118	173	188	79
Kezi	75 000	9 653	91	879	106	150	198	81
Plumtree	121 000	15 042	908	106	240	240	218	78
						921	894	474

Table 6 (continued)

District	Population	Families	Villages	Persons per village	Families per village	Village health workers Previous estimate	Village health workers Current estimate	Number trained
MIDLANDS								
Charter	97 000	22 559	136	1 118	166	193	193	76
Gokwe	227 000	46 951	232	1 159	202	477	477	85
Gwaru	47 000	7 691	69	841	111	93	93	86
Others: A	110 000	14 346	121	1 008	120	218	218	72
B	151 000	27 224	193	1 031	142	301	320	82
C	42 000	6 640	44	1 000	151	84	88	88
D	42 000	7 857	54	1 019	146	83	83	76
E	6 000	11 430	83	1 036	138	110	166	92
						1 559	1 638	657
VICTORIA								
Bikita	135 000	21 876	131	1 023	167	266	262	85
Chibi	138 000	32 683	156	885	210	275	275	87
Chiredzi	63 000	10 438	107	664	98	125	125	95
Gufu	177 000	26 551	228	1 048	116	350	300	105
Masvinge	117 000	18 614	196	638	95	231	210	103
Zaks	138 000	36 218	214	1 033	179	276	276	87
						1 523	1 448	562

(c) Place of treatment (percentage distribution):

Place of treatment	Female	Male
Health facility	72	55
Home	9	23
Other	3	3
None	16	19

(d) Distance from facility by place of treatment (percentage distribution):

Distance (km)	Number of health facilities	Number of homes
5	70	30
6 and above	30	70

(e) Maternal and child care:

   (i) 8 per cent of women's visits were for ante-natal care. Once a woman began ante-natal care, she tended to go more than once;

   (ii) 9 per cent of births were registered. This suggested that the pilot birth registration scheme was not working well.

Mr. Mkai pointed out, however, that the data showing only 9 per cent utilizing traditional healers was suspect, as respondents might be giving answers they thought the interviewer wanted.

In the general discussion, the following points were made:

(a) On health statistics:

   (i) It was essential to develop health indicators more relevant to the rural areas than the infant and maternal mortality rates;

   (ii) Ratios, such as the physician/population ratio, indicated availability but not access. To know whether women and girls had access to health providers, one needed to have utilization data;

   (iii) A health information module of the household survey programme should consider including questions on the following:

   a. Source of water;

   b. Type of waste disposal;

   c. Food consumption and nutritional status;

        d. Maternal and child health, and child-spacing knowledge, attitude, practice;

        e. Incidence and prevalence of infectious diseases;

        f. Incidence and prevalence of special local diseases;

        g. Treatment of common diseases;

        h. Availability and use of essential drugs;

        i. Mental health;

        j. Dental health;

(iv) Budgetary figures could provide important information about the priorities given to health and to particular services, such as maternal and child health and child-spacing services;

(v) Confusion often resulted when several different sets of figures purporting to measure the same thing were published. It was important to pinpoint the agency responsible for producing official estimates, and other agencies should use that agency's data. Where that agency had not yet published official figures, it was suggested that figures from other sources be labelled "provisional";

(vi) The Statistical Office of the United Nations Secretariat and the World Health Organization (WHO) might consider preparing a simple manual on health indicators, including terminology, formulas, methods of calculation, interpretation, use and limitations;

(b) On policy impact of health data in other sectors:

(i) Health statistics were important inputs into policy in other areas. For example, data on infant mortality and the interaction of undernutrition and communicable diseases, when combined with agricultural data showing that a change in traditional cropping patterns was reducing the per capita amount of maize available below the amount needed to maintain an adequate nutrition, led to a change in agricultural policy in Zimbabwe. In another example, health data were being used by the Ministry of Lands in planning for water and sanitation in Zimbabwe;

(ii) Information on specific diseases could point to problems within the jurisdiction of ministries other than the Ministry of Health. Interministerial communication and co-operation were essential for improving health. For example, in some areas goiter was an important female-related disease which could easily be prevented by using iodized salt, but the decision to treat salt lay outside the Ministry of Health.

In the following session, participants reconvened in their small working groups to complete the exercises on health status and health service indicators.

F. Women's organization

The afternoon session of the fifth day was devoted to consideration of indicators of women's organization and participation in political activities. The representatives of INSTRAW and the ECA/African Training and Research Centre for Women (ECA/ACTRCW), Ms. Tallawy and Ms. Hafkin, introduced the subject. The representative of INSTRAW began by describing some of the activities undertaken by international organizations to facilitate the participation of women in development. Within the United Nations system, INSTRAW, in co-operation with the International Labour Organisation, would conduct a series of regional studies on the participation of women in economic activities. A global analytical summary with projections to the year 2000 was planned.* Issues to be addressed included size and geographical distribution of the female population, levels and trends in female labour force participation by age, economic sector, occupation, status in employment, hours of work, employment, unemployment and other characteristics. The objectives were to facilitate development of policies to ensure equality of opportunity and treatment, to promote equality of opportunity and treatment of the women worker, to promote the measurement of women's economic contribution to development and to stimulate a re-orientation of development planning and strategies to include explicit consideration of women's participation in development.

A second project was under way, in co-operation with the Economic Commission for Latin America and the Caribbean (ECLAC), to assess the adequacy of questions currently being used in household survey programmes in eliciting information on women's economic roles in the household and labour market. The objective was to develop specific suggestions for improved data collection and to test them in the field.

INSTRAW was also assisting countries in establishing women's organizations and in preparing training materials for distribution to women's organizations to help them identify what information they needed. There was a need to strengthen women's organizations through the provision of qualified staff and adequate information. Research groups were also being established.

Many organizations outside the United Nations system were also active. The objectives were the same: to help women to carry out their roles in development more effectively. Methods were becoming more scientific and research-based. Organizations were tackling the broad economic issues facing developing societies and their work was practical and concrete. Many were producing directories or rosters of active women, organizations, resources and so on.

These activities and groups would come together at the Nairobi Conference, but it would be up to the national delegations to take the next step - to define what women's organizations needed next. Ms. Tallawy urged participants to communicate their concerns for active liaison with central statistical offices, more adequate information and more financial and human resources in statistical offices and women's organizations to obtain and use that information.

---

* The summary was subsequently published as <u>Women in Economic Activity: A Global Statistical Survey (1950-2000)</u> (Santo Domingo, ILO and INSTRAW, 1985).

The representative of ECA/ATRCW, Ms. Hafkin, reminded participants of the variety of women's organizations active at the national level. One goal of the United Nations Decade for Women was to promote the establishment within the Government of each country of a national machinery for the integration of women in development. The machinery was to operate as part of the national planning and budgeting process. Some countries, such as Mauritius and Zimbabwe, had established a separate ministry for women's issues. Others, such as Botswana, Kenya or Malawi, had established units or departments within a ministry.

A second way women had organized was through a wing of the national political party or other mass organizations. Zambia provided an example of that approach. The women's wing of UNIP, the national party, played a key role. Other examples included Ethiopia and Somalia. Women's non-governmental organizations of many different types constituted the third way in which women had organized to improve their participation in development. In Kenya, Maendelelo ya Wanawake served as a very effective umbrella organization for scores of smaller non-governmental organizations and for many development projects.

ECA/ATRCW was making information available to those organizations in a number of ways. It had issued a <u>Directory of National Machineries</u>, <u>Directory of Resources for Training for Women</u>, <u>Guide to Sources of Fund Raising</u> and <u>Guide to Project Development and Implementation</u>. Many countries had produced similar publications at the national level.

It was important to identify the kinds of information that would be most useful to grass-roots women's organizations and to be imaginative and creative in seeing how national women's organizations could assist local community groups. She pointed out that one of the objectives of the seminar's field trip (see annex IV) was to stimulate participants' thinking about the kinds of statistics and indicators that would be concretely useful to community projects themselves, and to those who would assist them. How might they be assisted by better data in project design and proposal development, in project monitoring and evaluation and in planning future activities? What data did they need to collect themselves as distinct from what they could obtain from a central statistical office or from a national women's organization? Women's organizations might undertake a survey on attitudes of men towards women's participation in literacy and income-generating campaigns, or a time-budget study that could lead to a project in appropriate technology. On the other hand, the central statistical office could provide information on female income, literacy, health and the like. An applied research unit within the national women's organization was needed to supplement the activities of the central statistical office.

Ms. Hafkin also underscored Ms. Tallawy's remarks about the importance of the Nairobi Conference, urging participants to contact their delegates about the need to strengthen material on statistics and indicators in the Forward-looking Strategies.

Discussants included Ms. Gladys Mulindi (Kenya), Ms. Godisang Mookodi (Botswana) and Ms. Kelemework Tekle (Ethiopia).

Ms. Mulindi noted that in Kenya there were more than 50,000 women's groups of more than 15 members recorded in the Women's Bureau: a directory was available.

There were also many smaller groups but the number was unknown. Maendeleo ya Wanawake listed about 300,000 members in December 1984. An umbrella group for non-governmental organizations, Maendeleo caters to women at the grass-roots level. National and non-political, it was founded in 1952, and more than 50 per cent of the women's non-governmental organizations were members. Along with the national executive committee, national chairman and central office, Maendeleo had representation at provincial, district, sub-location, location and village levels. There was a small paid staff but most activities were carried out by volunteers. The organization complements the development activities of the Government. Programmes include literacy, maternal and child health/family planning, home economics, income-generation, leadership training, energy, water and sanitation, and so on. Some programmes were funded by external donors.

Ms. Mookodi described the mission of the Women's Affairs Unit of the Ministry of Home Affairs in Botswana. The Ministry served to integrate women in every aspect of the development of the country and worked with other ministries, women's organizations and unorganized women. The Unit, founded in 1981, was relatively new and very small. There was also an interministerial committee to advise the several ministries on policies affecting women. Several of the larger women's non-governmental organizations (such as YWCA and the Botswana Council of Women) were registered with the Ministry of Home Affairs, but there were many smaller groups that were not registered. No directory of women's groups was available yet, nor did they have a mechanism to survey the many informal groups, so that although the Ministry had held two district-level seminars to try to reach local women's groups, the invitations did not reach them. However, the Ministry was still trying to reach those groups.

Ms. Hafkin suggested in response that the Unit design a questionnaire about women's groups and send it out with community development officers and extension personnel with some incentive for them to identify such groups in the areas they served. If funds were needed to publish a directory, application might be made to the Voluntary Fund through the United Nations Development Programme (UNDP).

Ms. Tekle described the role REWA, a party organization, was playing in integrating women in development. Established in 1980, it was organized at the commune, province, district, region and central levels. Activities included training in skills and literacy, development projects, co-operatives, public service (such as forestry and roads), cultural activities and study groups. Of 9.4 million women in the country aged 15 and over in 1984, 55 per cent were members of REWA. Of the 321,197 women who had been elected to work on REWA programmes, 100,000 of them worked full time. As a result of the literacy programme, 51 per cent of women were now literate. There was an urgent need for better statistics and for training in the generation and use of statistics and indicators.

In the discussion that followed, participants described the organization, structure and activities of their national women's agencies. In Kenya, the women's bureau was in the Department of Social Services. Women were represented on each of the District Development Committees and there were 25 workers who co-ordinated programmes in the field. They had received assistance from donor organizations in research, training and the establishment of an Information Unit within the Women's Bureau. Uganda had a National Council of Women to co-ordinate the activities of the many women's non-governmental organizations. Somalia's ruling party had a women's wing which worked with other women's organizations. It reached down to the village level.

In the United Republic of Tanzania, the Secretary-General of the national women's organization was a member of the National Executive Committee of the ruling Party, which was the highest policy-making body in the country. Women participated in other organizations, including co-operatives, the National Co-operative Union of Tanzania, the Young Women's Christian Association (YWCA) and other religious organizations. In Zambia, the Women's League of UNIP had been active since the time of the liberation struggle. It was a mass organization, mobilizing women for political, social and economic activities. A General Council met every five years; the National Council met annually. There was a National Executive Committee and chairmen at every level, from province to rural communities. They had an active research bureau. When they needed information, they might conduct their own study. They also worked closely with the central statistical office and non-governmental organizations and sought assistance from international donors for training, research and publication of materials.

The problem of co-ordinating the work of non-governmental organizations with the national women's organization was a recurrent theme. Registration and reporting requirements and consultative councils were two common mechanisms for co-ordination, but they had not been wholly satisfactory in the view of several participants. Finally, many stressed the importance of remaining sensitive and responsive to the needs and perspectives of rural women in organizing and mobilizing their participation in development activities.

G. Political participation

The representative of the Statistical Office of the United Nations Secretariat, Ms. Vanek, introduced the discussion of the measurement of women's political participation. She noted that although political participation could be a key indicator of the full participation of women in the decisions of the society, few statistics were available for the field. She suggested the following statistics and indicators:

(a) Women in government, at each level:

 (i) Numbers of women and men in ministerial positions, by type of ministry;

 (ii) Numbers of women and men who are members of national, provincial legislatures (appointed, elected);

 (iii) Numbers of women and men in the judicial system;

 (iv) Numbers of women and men among civil servants; proportion professional, managerial;

(b) Women in non-governmental but political structures:

 (i) Numbers of women and men in political parties;

 (ii) Numbers of women and men in trade unions;

 (iii) Number and type of women's organizations;

(c) Women's and men's voting.

Sources of data on political participation included government parliamentary records, government personnel data, registration of voters and membership lists of trade unions and other organizations. It was difficult to obtain data on voting behaviour because of the use of secret ballots. Data might come from sample surveys before the election and from exit polls.

Ms. Vanek gave an illustration of indicators of political participation by an analysis of the limited data available on women's membership in national legislatures from 1974-1985 for countries in the subregion. Data for China, the Soviet Union and the United States were given for the sake of comparison. The data showed low levels of participation and little change over time (percentages):

Country	Year	Percentage	Year	Percentage
Kenya	1974	2	1983	2
Malawi	1976	5	1983	9
Zambia	1978	4	1983	3
Zimbabwe	1981	7	1984	8
China	1975	23	1983	21
USSR	1974	32	1984	32
USA	1975	4	1983	4

Ms. Tallawy underscored Ms. Vanek's presentation, pointing out that it was not only in the seminar subregion that parliamentary participation was low. There were no women serving on the International Court of Justice, the United Nations Commission on Human Rights or the Joint Inspection Unit of the United Nations.

During the general discussion, the importance of having committed women in high places was illustrated by an account of how a shift in Zimbabwe's personnel policies had come about. Two lines of evidence showing the effective exclusion of women from decision-making had had tremendous impact. The first came from the Ministry of Community Development and Women's Affairs which had developed figures showing that only 9 per cent of the lower and 5 per cent of the upper legislative body were women. There was also a feeling that the number of women members of parliament was declining. At the local authority level, the first woman member of the Public Service Commission went through the Civil Service records in 1980 and found that, although women occupied 44.2 per cent of the salaried posts, they made up only 9 per cent of the senior officers. A strongly worded memo to all ministries from the Public Service Commission suggesting that people might have been passed over had increased awareness of the need to provide opportunities in government for women at senior levels.

In Malawi, the League of Malawi Women had promoted political participation as well as rural development. They had achieved some gains in the number of women, both elected and appointed, in the legislature.

Several participants noted the still more difficult problem of encouraging rural women to stand for election to political office or to office in farmers' co-operatives or other organizations.

The discussion closed on a note of caution. In interpreting statistics on female voters it was important to remember that although women's votes had been counted for a long time, women were rarely part of the decision-making cadre. Voting <u>per se</u> was not a good indicator of full participation. It was also important to remember that lists of registered voters were often inflated.

III. NEEDS AND PROSPECTS FOR IMPROVING STATISTICS AND
INDICATORS ON WOMEN IN DEVELOPMENT

(Seventh day of the programme)*

A. National programmes

During the second session of the final day of the seminar, attention was given to national programmes to improve statistics and indicators of women's integration into development. Three kinds of national programmes were considered:

(a) Programmes to develop national data bases on women;

(b) Programmes for dissemination of statistics and indicators to user organizations and the general public;

(c) Programmes to improve the utilization of statistics and indicators on women in policy development and programme planning, monitoring and evaluation.

1. Data base development and dissemination

The representative of the Statistical Office of the United Nations, Ms. Vanek, introduced the discussion of data base development and dissemination of statistics, using the data base developed at the Statistical Office as an illustration of what might be done at a national level. There were five steps in creating a data base:

(a) Review data developed by other organizations and available literature for ideas about what indicators to include;

(b) Specify what variables one wants to measure;

(c) Decide how best to present those variables as indicators of the situation of women: percentage of total, percentage of women, female/male ratio, etc.;

(d) Where feasible, use measures that facilitate international comparison;

(e) Wherever possible, use rural/urban breakdowns.

Since the objective was to make data more accessible to users, it was important to ensure that the output from the data bases was widely disseminated. In June 1985, the United Nations issued a document prepared by the Statistical Office for the Nairobi Conference entitled "Selected statistics and indicators on the status of women", using data from the Statistical Office data base in six fields:

---

* The sixth day of the programme was devoted to field visits, which are discussed in annex IV.

-67-

(a) Population composition, distribution and change;

(b) Education, training and literacy;

(c) Economic activity;

(d) Households, marital status and fertility;

(e) Health and nutrition;

(f) Political participation.

Eventually those data would be available on diskettes for use by interested countries.

The representative of INSTRAW underscored the importance of data base development and dissemination of information. It was particularly important to have national data on rural women. She informed participants that INSTRAW and the ILO were also completing a publication for the Nairobi Conference in the labour force. She pointed out that dissemination was a special responsibility in the Africa region, where communication was difficult.

Discussants for the two topics were Mr. Cletus Mkai (United Republic of Tanzania) and Mr. D. Ahawo (Kenya). Mr. Mkai recounted his country's experience in developing a data base and an information dissemination programme. They proceeded in six steps, similar to those described by Ms. Vanek:

(a) Review of publications and the experience of others, notably Botswana and Kenya;

(b) Meeting of Central Statistical Office staff with users, especially users who collected data;

(c) Review of sources of data;

(d) Development of a strategy to sensitize data collection systems to gather data on women;

(e) Workshops to decide on which indicators to include, followed by consultation with users to refine the list. Users included:

(i) Planners in the sectoral ministries who wanted better social indicators;

(ii) Other analysts who performed research or lectured in social statistics;

(iii) Parastatals;

(f) Workshops to present recommendations, which included:

(i) Publish Annual and give a five-year series;

-68-

- (ii) Disaggregate statistics by region, age, sex, plus other relevant characteristics;

- (iii) Assign statistical officers to produce readable, well-written statistical reports:

    a. First drafts of selected chapters to be written by other resource persons;

    b. Reports to be sent to users for review;

    c. Editorial workshop to discuss draft before final report is issued;

- (iv) Attend to the content and style of publications:

    a. If statistical terminology is used, add definitions;

    b. Stress that these are indicators, not absolute values;

    c. Use graphs and charts with text underneath; use few elaborate tables.

Mr. Ahawo noted that the growing concern for social justice had added new responsibilities to statistical offices. They must develop a barometer for measuring social justice. With the decentralization of planning in Kenya to the district level, the challenge was to localize statistical information on women in each district to incorporate women into district development plans. In addition to publishing three volumes on women in Kenya, they intended to hold a national workshop similar to the present one to promote dialogue between producers and users.

Ms. Vanek remarked in closing that women were a new group of users and that they must establish their credibility with central statistical offices. The more women could show that their demands for data were based on research or on a wide review of opinion, the more attention that demand was likely to receive. Users must also recognize that central statistical offices faced many competing demands. The Central Statistical Office, for its part, needed to stay in contact with users and find new ways to meet user needs. Flexibility, openness and a willingness to continue the dialogue were called for on both sides.

2. Statistics and indicators in programme and policy planning

Ms. Elias introduced the subject of programme and policy planning by describing the training programme which she directed at the Eastern and Southern Africa Management Institute (ESAMI) entitled "Developmental planning, management, and women". The objectives of the programme were:

(a) To increase the awareness on the part of planners, economists and experts in development policy, both men and women, about the role of women in development;

(b) To provide participants with tools and skills which would make their work in planning, management and evaluation more effective.

The strategy developed at ESAMI focused on women's participation as a development issue and included both men and women, so that women's contribution to development became more than a concern of women alone. Moreover, the result of the sharing and dialogue during the course was a plan of action, oriented towards influencing policy. Such a plan was developed by each participant country group. Since 1981, 107 individuals (80 women, 27 men) from 14 countries had participated in the course.

The results of the five-year programme, which had been positive on the whole, included the following:

(a) More men were aware of women's participation as a development issue;

(b) A series of action plans were at various stages of implementation (for example, statistical and data collection instruments at the district level in Kenya had been modified to indicate beneficiaries and participants in development programmes);

(c) There was more commitment at a personal level;

(d) Technical competence had improved;

(e) An increasing number of female participants had sought further training;

(f) There was increased awareness within ESAMI of women's roles as a development issue.

At ESAMI they were alert to ways in which their training programmes might influence policy, such as:

(a) Increasing the number of women professionals;

(b) Encouraging participation of women in:

(i) Regular management training programmes;

(ii) Special seminars for women managers;

(c) Developing more awareness on the part of women professionals of women's roles in development;

(d) Including sessions on women and work within the regular management programmes;

(e) Inspiring other management programmes to address topics of importance to women managers and entrepreneurs;

(f) Developing a dialogue between researchers and planners so that research leads to changes in policy.

In the discussion, a number of questions were asked about how to measure the impact of programmes such as that of ESAMI. Many felt that while participants from their countries had personally benefited from the programme, it had not yet had wide impact on policy development. However, such a programme might be a useful first step.

B. Conclusions

The Technical Co-ordinator opened the final session with a review of the accomplishments of the Seminar relative to the objectives initially set for it. They were:

(a) To facilitate a dialogue between producers and users about demand for and sources and applications of statistics and indicators on women in development;

(b) To familiarize participants with ways in which data, statistics and indicators of women's situation were currently being collected, compiled and used in the region;

(c) To provide experience in calculating, presenting and interpreting a representative set of statistics and indicators on women;

(d) To contribute to an ongoing search for better ways of incorporating data on women into national statistical series and of using such data in policy and programme planning.

She noted that during the meeting many producers of statistics had shared information on their accomplishments and problems in trying to provide accurate and timely statistics to serve national needs for policy development, planning, monitoring and evaluation. Users discussed their needs for data, some of the ways in which those needs had been met, and their frustrations in trying to get certain kinds of information, pointing to the gaps yet to be filled.

In the closing session, the time had come to consider the future. That session would review some of the most important of the unmet data needs discussed and consider the prospects for development of adequate statistics and indicators on women in the subregion. To help guide the closing discussion, each of six panel members had been asked to summarize some of the important points made during the earlier sessions and to make suggestions for the future.

Maintaining that existing data series could provide sufficient information for planning, monitoring and evaluating women's participation in development provided planners were prepared to take women seriously, Ms. Makonnen (Ethiopia) stressed the importance of making the demand for statistics on women unmistakably clear. She urged that participants contact statisticians in their home countries and lobby to have the Conference of African Planners, Statisticians and Demographers address the need for better data on women. They should be urged to support the position that statistics on women constituted a deliberate and distinct component of statistical reporting and that planning for national development should include explicit attention to women. She also reminded producers that inasmuch as many errors of bias and misinterpretation originated in the field-work, instruction programmes and manuals for interviewers should be prepared very carefully.

Ms. Mbere (Botswana) stressed the importance of small-scale and special surveys to supplement national data programmes. Such data were particularly important in understanding the needs of the informal sector and of the rural population, especially at the district or community levels. Small-scale surveys could help to decentralize data collection and might even involve village people in participatory research. In those efforts, it was important to remain flexible and open to new research methods. Ms. Mbere reported success in Botswana in using video to compare the performance of traditional birth attendants and modern midwives and to assess training needs. Addressing the need for information dissemination, she noted that effective dissemination of results started in pre-project consultations and was made more likely by ongoing consultation during the research, so that others became involved in the outcome while the study was still under way.

Ms. Mzelethe (Zimbabwe) stressed the interaction of small studies with the population census and other national data systems. For example, small-scale research could be guided by the census in designing the study and constructing a sampling frame, while the census could be improved by the results of individual research projects. Administrative statistics, too, needed much improvement and could benefit from special studies. For any given purpose it was important to decide which activities could best be carried out by the Central Statistical Office and which were best left to administrative departments, other user organizations or universities and research institutes. A centralized repository was also needed, where results could be received and information co-ordinated. Ms. Mzelethe reminded participants that although better statistics and indicators were necessary, they would not in themselves bring about improvement in the situation of women in the household and society. Such improvement called for changes in social and political attitudes and behaviour.

Ms. Yoyo (Zambia) expressed appreciation for the efforts of central statistical offices. She reminded participants that the offices faced heavy and sometimes conflicting demands and were frequently overburdened. She suggested that there should be an ongoing dialogue to develop additional ways of collecting data on women. That was not to suggest that the national statistical series need not include information on women but rather to stress the importance of the research initiatives of women's organizations in assisting women to become more effective participants in all aspects of development, not merely the social and cultural aspects.

Mr. Mkai (United Republic of Tanzania) expressed optimism at the prospects for an improved data base on women. Even now, useful data came from national censuses, and national household survey programmes were becoming more sophisticated in obtaining information about household members. Many were eager to strengthen administrative statistics, although that was more difficult. He suggested that the participants begin seminars similar to this one in their own countries, with discussion and data analysis directed towards areas of national policy interest. He closed by pointing out that "today's participants may be tomorrow's policy makers".

Mr. Tichagwa (Zimbabwe) urged that each user organization be encouraged to make the collection of information on women an important part of its activities. He also stressed the importance of feeding back statistics and information to the grass-roots level.

In the ensuing discussion the following points were made:

(a) On follow-up national seminars:

    (i) It was important to follow up the subregional seminar with in-country workshops and seminars. Perhaps a questionnaire could go to each ministry to find out what information was available and how its programme affected women;

    (ii) In-country seminars must not preach to the already converted. It was not a struggle between women and men. Even the most stubborn men were beginning to see that they could not afford a development strategy where 50 per cent of those of working age were not considered productive. Women *were* participating in development, but demographers and planners needed to be made aware of the unrecorded work women were doing and to develop policies and programmes to make that work more efficient. It was important that men participate in in-country seminars;

    (iii) In conducting a seminar such as the current one, one might consider organizing the format around a series of problems to solve. The exercises would be directed towards using available data in the solution of the particular problem posed. For example, let us say the question was "How do we find out about levels of income which women in income-generating projects receive?" The exercises would focus on what information was available, how to design a study to obtain other data, how to compile a set of relevant indicators, and the policy implications of the findings;

    (iv) It would be useful to have additional indicators on health and nutrition in future seminars. Perhaps "average number of months of breast-feeding" would prove to be a useful indicator of the risk of high maternal and child mortality. Perhaps indicators on cooking-fuel consumption or feeding patterns could be developed;

(b) On other follow-up activities:

    (i) Perhaps the United Nations could sponsor a Statistical Decade for 1986-1995, to improve techniques and develop a better set of social and economic indicators;

    (ii) Some machinery for co-ordination was essential if data generated by a variety of agencies were to be fully utilized;

    (iii) Umbrella women's organizations could help local women by assisting them to determine the feasibility of proposed income-generating projects. Successful projects could be stepping-stones to a better life for rural women;

(c) On specific tabulations:

   (i) There was a trade-off between developing relevant country-specific indicators and using indicators that were comparable across countries. Perhaps two sets of tabulations for selected indicators might be necessary;

   (ii) Users must be very clear about the information they requested from the Central Statistical Office and be realistic about the feasibility of obtaining it.

Exercise I

POPULATION

A. Population structure and change

1. Complete exercise table 1. For the growth rate, use the first method of computing an annual growth rate described below.

2. Discuss the uses and limitations for national planning of the following indicators from the table: (a) the dependency ratio, (b) the child/woman ratio.

_____
_____
_____
_____

3. Discuss the implications for national planning of the following indicators from the table: (a) the median age of this population, (b) the annual rate of growth of this population.

_____
_____
_____
_____

(a) **How to estimate an annual rate of growth**

There are several ways one can estimate an annual rate of growth. Formulas for three different methods are given below, in order of increasing computational difficulty and accuracy. The first formula simply computes the total percentage growth over a period of time and divides by the number of years in the period. The second assumes that the population base is larger each year. It adds the new people at the end of each year, then multiplies by the annual rate of growth. This is identical to the way a bank figures interest on savings when they compound the interest once a year. The third formula also assumes that the population base is growing but it adds the new people continuously, not just once a year.

Exercise table 1. Population structure and change: Population by age and sex and sex ratios, United Republic of Tanzania, 1967

Age group	Male	Female	Total	Sex ratio (males/100 females)	Female share (%)	Cumulative total
0-4	1 090 990	1 114 911	2 205 901	97.9	50.5	2 205 901
5-9	976 427	968 180	1 944 607	100.9	49.8	4 150 508
10-14	657 147	590 866	1 248 013	111.2	47.3	5 398 521
15-19	512 657	570 595	1 083 252	89.8	52.1	6 481 773
20-24	378 435	542 974	921 409	69.7	58.9	7 403 182
25-29	461 270	572 000	1 033 270	80.6	55.4	8 436 452
30-34	358 608	401 795	760 403	89.3	52.8	9 196 855
35-39	341 101	334 742	675 843	----	----	9 872 698
40-44	221 936	236 334	458 270	----	----	10 330 968
45-49	252 613	231 284	483 897	----	----	10 814 865
50-54	178 102	183 571	361 673	----	----	11 176 538
55-59	108 992	102 632	211 624	----	----	11 388 162
60-64	110 566	117 424	227 990	----	----	11 616 152
65+	364 027	320 161	684 188	----	----	12 300 340
Unknown	3 141	2 604	5 745	----	----	12 306 085
Total	6 016 012	6 290 073	12 306 085	----	----	----

Source: United Republic of Tanzania, Bureau of Statistics, _1967 Population Census_, vol. 3, _Demographic Statistics_ (Dar es Salaam, 1970).

Total less than age 15: _____ = _____ %
Total aged 60 and over: _____ = _____ %
Total aged 65 and over: _____ = _____ %
Total dependent population: _____ = _____ %
Total working age population: _____ = _____ %
"Dependency ratio": _____ = _____ %

Children under age 5: _____
Women aged 15-49: _____
Child/woman ratio: _____

Median age: _____

Annual rate of growth calculation:

	Male	Female	Total
1967	6 016 012	6 290 073	12 306 085
1968	8 595 951	8 931 613	17 527 564
Growth	----	----	----
Annual growth rate			----
Years to double			----

This is the formula for exponential growth. In the formulas, P_1 = population at the beginning of the period, P_2 = population at the end, n = number of years, r = annual rate of growth.

1. Average annual rate of growth: $r = (P_2 - P_1)/nP_1$

2. Annual growth rate, Compound interest formula: $P_2/P_1 = (1 + r)^n$

3. Annual growth rate, exponential growth formula: $P_2/P_1 = e^{rn}$.

(b) How to estimate years to double the population

From the exponential growth formula it is easy to compute the number of years it will take for the population to double, assuming the annual rate of growth is known and you have an estimate of r. In this case $e^{rn} = 2$, and r is known. Since the natural logarithm of 2 = 0.69, to solve for n (the years to double) divide 69 by r. That is, n = 69/r. For example, Kenya's estimated annual growth is 4 per cent. The estimated doubling time = 69/4 or 17.25 years.

B. Distribution of the population by marital status

1. Complete exercise table 2.

2. Describe the differences shown by the table in the age pattern of marriage for women and men.

_____
_____
_____
_____

3. Discuss the implications for policy and programme planning of these differences.

_____
_____
_____
_____
_____

Exercise table 2. Distribution of population by marital status: Total population 10 years old and over, by marital status, age and sex, United Republic of Tanzania, 1967

Sex and age group	Total	Single	Married	Widowed	Separated/ divorced
Total	8 149 596	2 516 725	4 891 741	399 618	329 846
Males	3 945 325	1 576 298	2 180 658	60 003	121 042
10-14	657 138	652 802	2 514	679	287
15-19	512 653	476 411	33 824	639	1 134
20-24	378 423	214 336	154 931	1 710	6 194
25-29	461 251	113 174	331 624	2 736	13 160
30-34	358 604	43 200	297 261	2 827	14 658
35-39	341 101	25 630	297 567	3 358	14 298
40-44	221 935	12 908	194 362	2 840	11 194
45-49	252 606	11 199	224 972	4 635	11 636
50-54	178 105	7 520	154 867	4 732	10 365
55-59	108 969	4 161	94 867	3 404	6 445
60-64	110 561	4 025	93 680	4 875	7 631
65+	363 979	10 932	300 189	27 568	24 040
Females	4 204 271	940 427	2 711 083	339 615	208 804
10-14	590 850	570 725	18 121	824	597
15-19	570 587	271 995	284 398	2 595	11 204
20-24	542 979	49 255	465 555	5 060	21 804
25-29	572 009	18 167	520 426	8 164	24 979
30-34	401 789	7 773	361 416	11 541	20 711
35-39	334 726	4 810	296 099	15 153	18 621
40-44	236 324	3 399	197 603	18 899	16 117
45-49	231 273	2 933	182 305	28 444	17 498
50-54	183 567	2 474	125 966	36 479	18 403
55-59	102 628	1 340	65 006	25 773	10 476
60-64	117 425	2 055	65 101	37 527	12 589
65+	320 114	5 501	129 087	149 156	35 805

Source: United Republic of Tanzania, Bureau of Statistics, 1967 Population Census, vol. 3, Demographic Statistics (Dar es Salaam, 1970), table 203.

Percentage single, ages 20-24 and 45-49, by sex:

	Aged 20-24 Number	Percentage	Aged 45-49 Number	Percentage
Males	----	----	----	----
Females	----	----	----	----
Female/male ratio		----		----

C. Household size

1. Complete exercise table 3, calculating the cumulative percentage distribution of households by household size and estimating household size at the upper limit of the third quartile (Q3), that is, the size below which 75 per cent of the households fall.

2. Complete exercise figure 1 on the cumulative percentage distribution.

3. How might this information be used for planning?

Exercise table 3. Household size: Population and households by household size, Zambia, 1969

Persons per household	Households Number	Cumulative Number	Cumulative Percentage	
1	107 322	107 322	12.3	
				Size at quartile 1 = 1.95 persons
2	130 008	237 330	27.2	
3	128 001	365 331	41.8	
				Median size = 3.59 persons
4	120 589	485 920	55.6	
5	102 603	588 523	----	
				Size at quartile 3 = 5.__ persons
6	86 421	674 944	----	
7	62 871	737 815	----	
8	58 851	796 666	----	
9	22 582	819 248	----	
10 and over	54 045	873 293	100.0	
Total	873 293	873 293	100.0	

Source: Zambia, Central Statistical Office, Census of Population and Housing, Final Report, vol. 1, Total Zambia (Lusaka, 1973), table 6.

Calculation of median household size:
   873293/2 = 436646.5; 436646.5 - 365331.0 = 71315.5
   71315.5/120589.0 = 0.59; Median size = 3.59 persons

Calculation of household size at first and third quartiles:
   873293/4 = 218323.25;
   Q1: 218323.25 - 107322.00 = 111001.25;
       111001.25/130008.00 = .85   Q1 = 1.85 persons
   Q3: 218323.25 * 3 = 654969.75; 654969.75 - 588523 = 66446.75
       66446.75/86421.00 = 0.77   Q3 = 5.__ persons

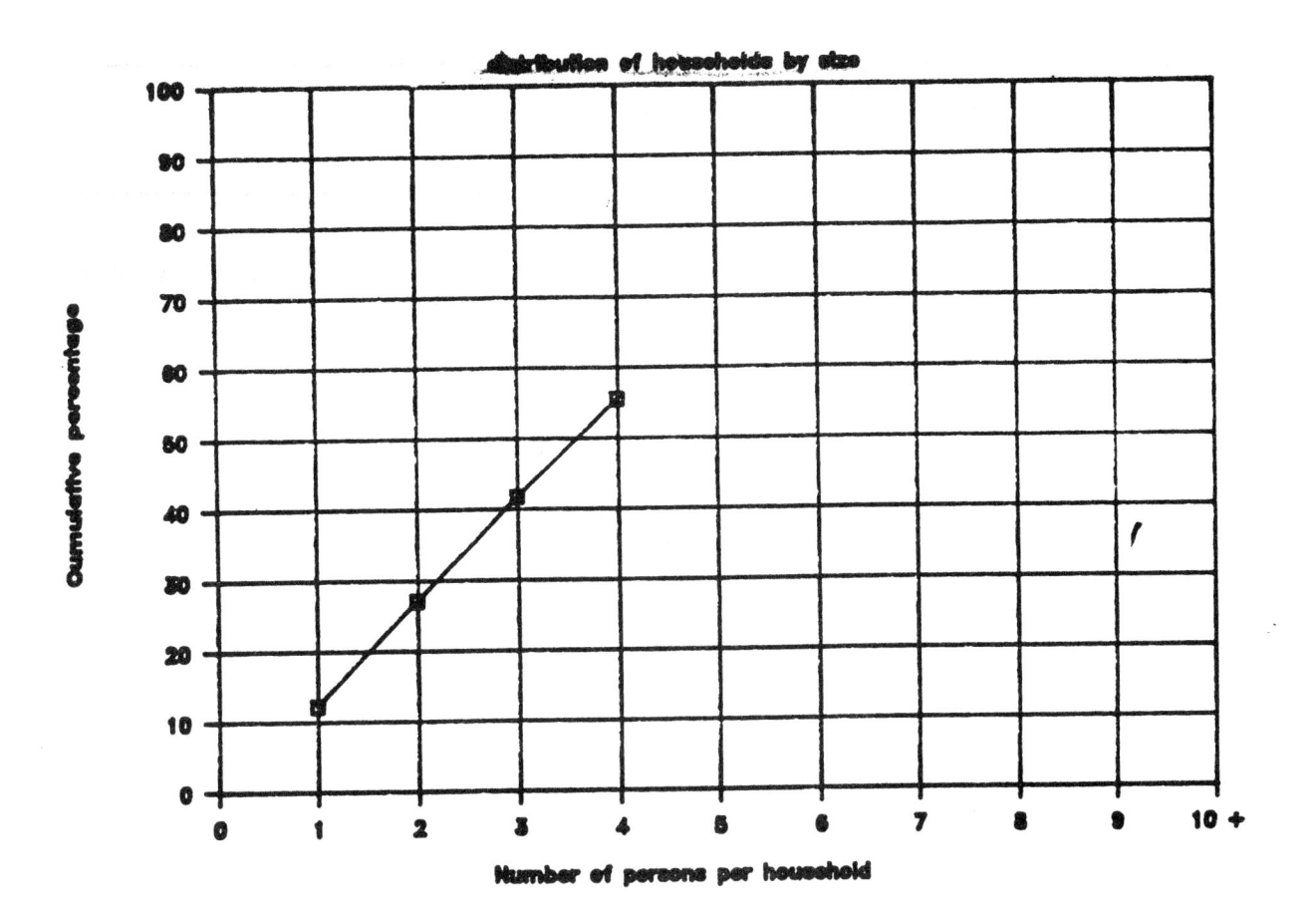

Exercise figure 1. Cumulative percentage distribution of households by size

-83-

D. Heads of households by sex and urban/rural residence

1. Complete exercise table 4.

2. Discuss some of the reasons why many believe the proportion of household heads who are women is underestimated.

___

3. How might one account for the differences between rural and urban areas in the proportion of households headed by women? What special problems might rural female-household heads face? How might they differ from those faced by urban female-household heads?

___

Exercise table 4. Heads of households, by sex and urban/rural residence, Sudan, 1973

	Number	Percentage	Female/male ratio
Total	2 288 277	100.0	
Male	1 781 491	----	
Female	506 786	22.1	0.28
Urban	472 746	100.0	
Male	393 340	83.2	
Female	79 406	16.8	0.20
Rural	1 815 531	100.0	
Male	1 388 151	76.5	
Female	427 380	----	----

Source: Sudan, Ministry of National Planning, Second Population Census, 1973, vol. 1, Socio-Economic Characteristics (Khartoum, 1977), table 24. Heads of households were enumerated as reported by household members. Data refer to settled population only.

E. Geographical mobility among women and men, by size of place

1. Complete exercise table 5.

2. Circle the peak age of mobility for women and for men in each type of settlement and for all movers, regardless of where they live.

3. Do you agree with those who say that geographical mobility is primarily a male phenomenon? What are the reasons for your answer?

_____
_____
_____
_____
_____
_____
_____

4. At what ages and in which types of settlements are there more female than male movers? Do you think this is merely because there are more females than males at these ages? What else would you need to know to answer this?

_____
_____
_____
_____
_____

Exercise table 5. Geographical mobility among women and men, by size of place: Movers by size of present locality of residence, sex and age, Botswana, 1981

Age group	Urban (>5000) Female	Urban (>5000) Male	Urban (>5000) Percentage female	Town (1000-5000) Female	Town (1000-5000) Male	Town (1000-5000) Percentage female	Village (<1000) Female	Village (<1000) Male	Village (<1000) Percentage female	Total Female	Total Male	Total Percentage female
0-4	1 854	1 753	51.4	1 894	1 841	50.7	4 323	4 237	50.5	8 071	7 831	50.8
5-9	2 236	1 748	56.1	2 258	1 853	54.9	6 798	6 806	50.0	11 292	10 407	52.0
10-14	2 401	1 357	----	2 441	1 583	----	7 884	8 518	----	12 726	11 458	----
15-19	4 118	2 928	----	3 842	2 328	----	5 567	5 483	----	13 527	10 739	----
20-24	3 799	4 013	----	3 343	2 599	----	4 086	3 712	----	11 228	10 324	----
25-34	3 321	4 489	----	3 540	3 584	----	4 956	5 511	----	11 817	13 584	----
35-44	1 308	2 035	39.1	1 525	1 967	43.7	2 877	3 616	44.3	5 710	7 618	42.8
45-54	774	977	44.2	954	1 172	44.9	2 208	2 517	46.7	3 936	4 606	45.8
55-64	534	492	50.0	654	751	46.5	1 593	1 764	47.4	2 781	3 007	48.0
65+	527	329	61.6	649	570	53.2	1 938	1 917	50.3	3 114	2 816	52.5
Unknown	156	229	40.5	129	188	40.7	513	558	47.9	298	975	45.0
Total	21 028	20 350	----	21 229	18 436	----	42 743	44 639	----	84 500	83 365	----

Source: Data compiled from Botswana 1981 population census.

F. Age distribution of fertility

1. Complete exercise table 6A, calculating the percentage change in the age-specific fertility rate in Lesotho between 1967-1971 and 1972-1976.

2. Would you say there has been much change in these rates during the decade 1967-1976? At which age do there appear to be the greatest differences between the two sets of rates? Why or why not do you think such large differences in those age groups are likely to be significant?

_____
_____
_____

3. Complete exercise table 6B, calculating the percentage of total lifetime fertility added during each age group.

4. From these data would you say that the age distribution of fertility has changed very much over the decade 1968-1977?

_____
_____
_____

5. Examine exercise figure 2A. Health authorities tell us that the lowest risk pregnancies occur in women between ages 20 and 35. What does this pie chart suggest about programme needs?

_____
_____
_____

6. Complete exercise figure 2B of children ever born by age of mother for the 1967/69 survey. At which age has fertility risen most steeply over the decade 1968-1977?

_____
_____
_____
_____
_____

Exercise table 6: Age distribution of fertility, 1967-1977, Lesotho

A. Age-specific fertility rates

Age group	Age-specific fertility rates (live births per 1000 women, annually)		Percentage change
	1967-1971	1972-1976	
15-19	82	103	--
20-24	244	261	+7
25-29	259	252	-3
30-34	216	233	+8
35-39	167	173	+4
40-44	108	95	--
45-49	(27)	27	--
Total fertility rate	5.52	5.72	+4

B. Mean number of children ever born by age of women

	1967/69 survey			1977 survey		
Age group	Mean number of children ever born per woman	Mean additional number of children born per woman	Percentage	Mean number of children ever born per woman	Mean additional number of children born per women	Percentage
15-19	0.12	0.12	3	0.19	0.19	3
20-24	1.08	0.96	20	1.27	1.08	20
25-29	2.44	1.36	---	2.50	1.23	---
30-34	3.63	1.19	---	3.90	1.40	---
35-39	4.36	0.73	15	4.66	0.76	14
40-44	4.76	0.40	8	5.08	0.42	8
45-49	4.78	0.02	---	5.40	0.32	---
Lifetime		4.78	100		5.40	100

Source: Ian Timaeus and K. Balasubramanian, *Evaluation of the Lesotho Fertility Survey, 1977*, Scientific Reports No. 58 (London, World Fertility Survey, August 1984), pp. 24-25.

Exercise figure 2. Age distribution of fertility, Lesotho

A. Lifetime percentage distribution

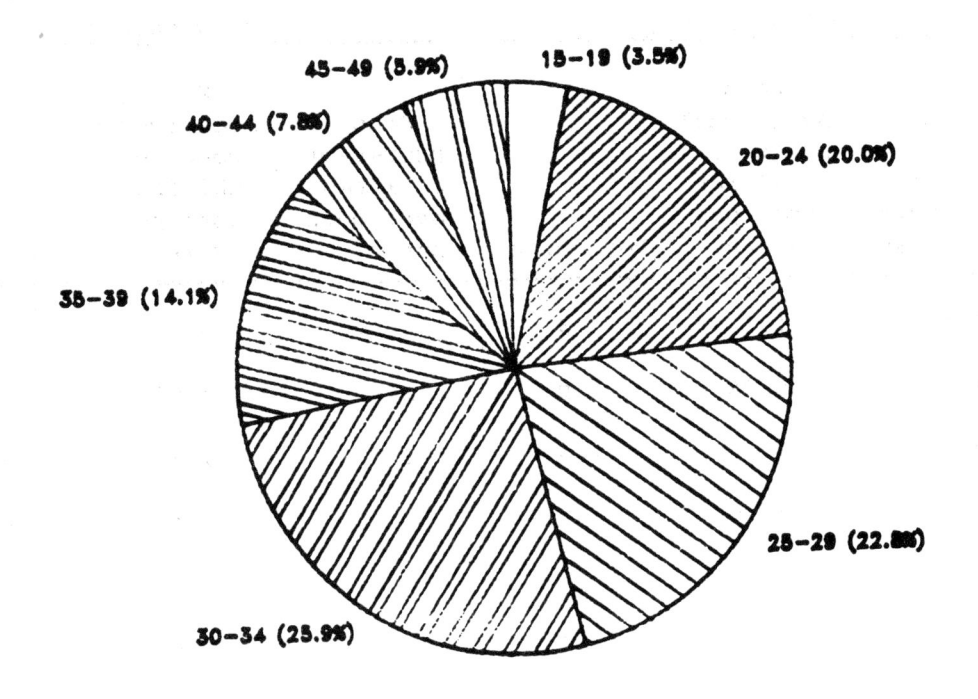

- 15-19 (3.5%)
- 20-24 (20.0%)
- 25-29 (22.8%)
- 30-34 (25.9%)
- 35-39 (14.1%)
- 40-44 (7.8%)
- 45-49 (5.9%)

B. Mean number of children ever born by age group

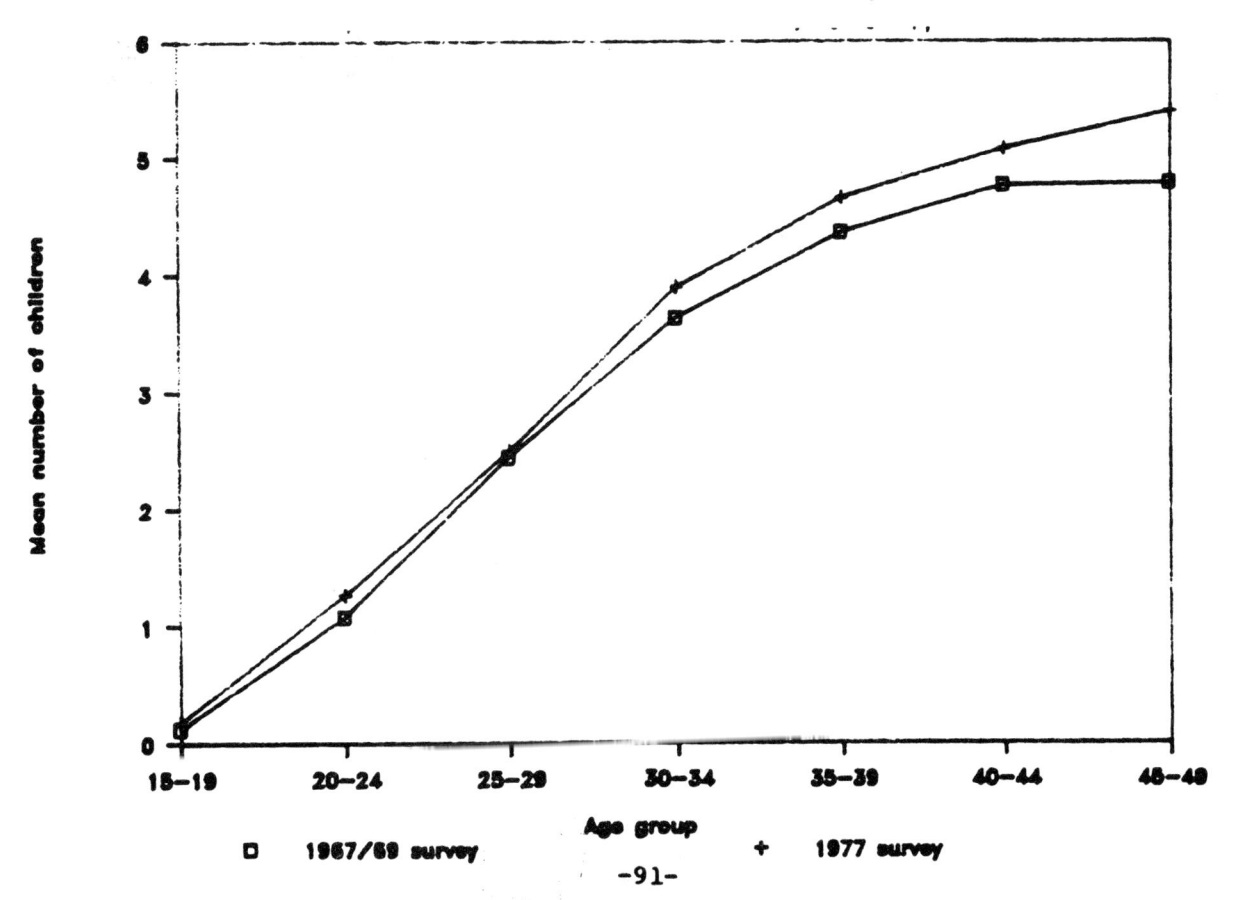

□ 1967/69 survey   + 1977 survey

Exercise figure 3. Literate (%), by age group and sex

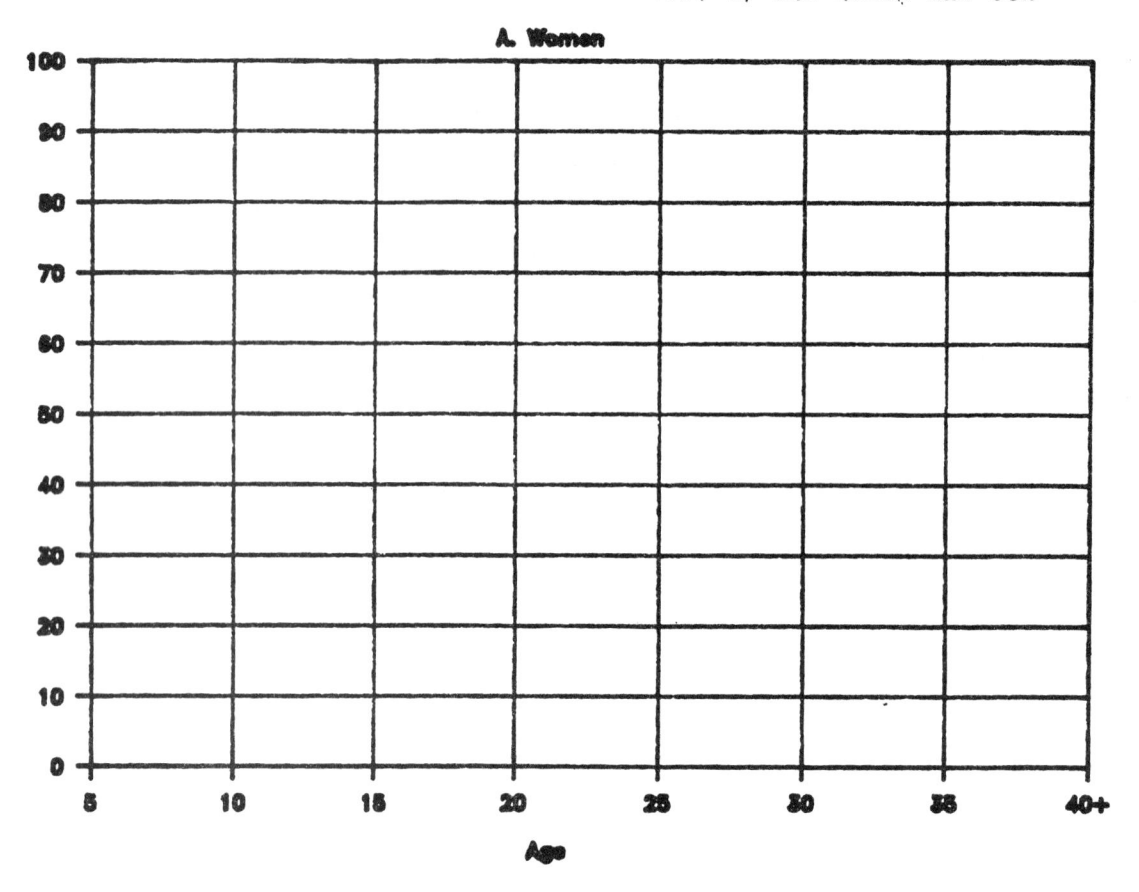

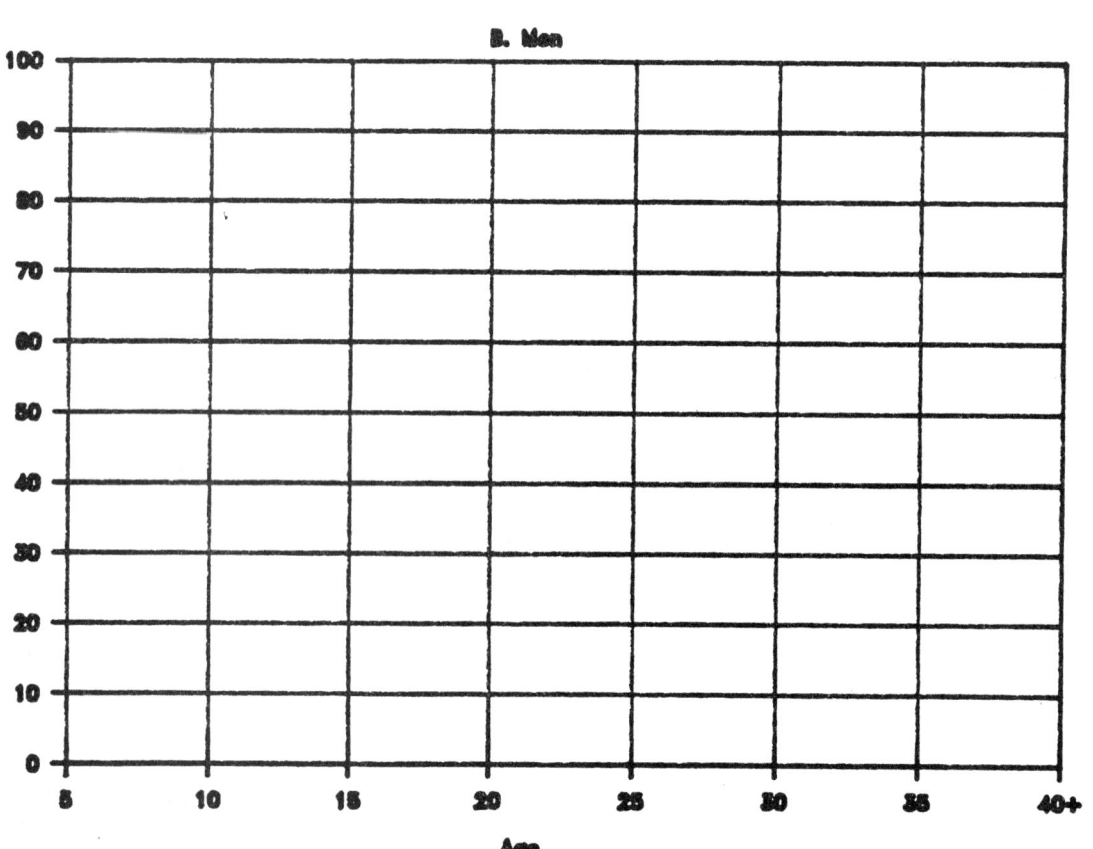

A. Women

B. Men

Exercise II

EDUCATION

A. Literacy of women and men

Exercise table 7 shows percentage literate by selected age groups and by sex for several sub-Saharan African countries.

1. Select two or three countries of interest and for each country plot the percentage literate by age for women and men on exercise figure 3.

2. Using data in table 7, compute female/male ratios of percentage literate for each age group for at least two countries:

Country: _____

Age group	Percentage literate Female	Male	Female/male ratio
10-14	_____	_____	_____
15-24	_____	_____	_____
25-34	_____	_____	_____
35+	_____	_____	_____

Country: _____

Age group	Female	Male	Female/male ratio
10-14	_____	_____	_____
15-24	_____	_____	_____
25-34	_____	_____	_____
35+	_____	_____	_____

3. Do you think these indicators suggest any trends in literacy over time? Discuss.

_____
_____
_____
_____

4. How might information on literacy be used in programme planning?

_____
_____
_____

Exercise table 7. Percentage literate by sex and age group

Region and country	Year	Female 10-14	Female 15-24	Female 25-34	Female 35 and over	Male 10-14	Male 15-24	Male 25-34	Male 35 and over
SAHEL WEST AFRICA									
Burkina Faso	1975	11.0	6.7	2.6	1.0	20.7	22.3	15.1	8.9
Cape Verde	1960	28.8	24.4	17.4	14.0	41.4	45.9	39.5	42.6
Mali	1960-61	4.7	1.5 a/	0.5 d/	0.0 c/	9.7	5.5 a/	4.6 b/	2.7 c/
COASTAL WEST AFRICA									
Benin	1961	..	3.9	1.5	0.6	..	14.5	7.1	4.8
Ghana	1971	..	39.6	14.3	5.0	..	68.6	46.6	22.7
Ivory Coast	1975	40.0	21.5	5.5	2.3	60.4	43.7	21.8	10.1
Liberia	1974	24.0	19.4	6.9	4.7	32.7	51.7	30.7	14.2
Sierra Leone	1963	13.4	5.6	3.1	4.1	24.2	22.1	14.0	9.6
Togo	1970	31.8 d/	16.8	5.5	2.1	60.5 d/	48.4	28.0	14.1
CENTRAL AFRICA									
Cameroon	1976	71.1	56.1	24.2	7.3	78.5	76.1	56.7	29.2
EASTERN AFRICA									
Ethiopia e/	1970	1.8	0.4	0.1	0.1	11.9	11.4	8.7	6.3
Mauritius	1962	62.0 f/	65.5 g/	49.5	38.0	67.2 f/	80.1 g/	70.1	65.3
Seychelles	1960	..	60.4	52.5	40.3	..	48.8	48.5	35.5
Sudan	1973	44.9	27.5	9.8	4.0	64.9	55.2	41.8	30.6
Tanzania	1967	42.5	29.4	13.9	4.9	56.3	60.3	49.3	29.4
SOUTHERN AFRICA									
Botswana	1964	49.7	52.5	39.8	21.1	32.7	39.3	33.9	23.6
Lesotho	1966	63.9	89.1	81.3	49.7	30.2	53.4	49.7	36.8
Mozambique	1970	20.9	11.7	6.1	4.3	26.9	24.9	20.0	12.4
Zambia	1969	75.6	60.3	33.2	13.7	79.4	82.5	70.3	43.9

Source: United States of America, Bureau of the Census, *Women of the World, Sub-Saharan Africa*, by Jeanne S. Newman, WID-2 (Washington, D.C., Government Printing Office, 1985), table 4.4.

a/ Aged 15-19.

b/ Aged 20-39.

c/ Aged 40 and over.

d/ Aged 12-14.

e/ Rural areas only.

f/ Aged 5-12.

g/ Aged 13-24.

B. School enrolment by grade/form

Even in Zimbabwe, where school enrolment of girls is relatively high, there are important differences in the school enrolment patterns of boys and girls. Exercise table 8 shows 1979 school enrolment in Zimbabwe by grade or form, separately for each sex and for all pupils. An "apparent enrolment rate" has been calculated for each grade/form, for primary and for secondary school.

1. Why do you think the Ministry calls these rates "apparent"? Another term than "apparent rate" might be _____

2. Complete the table by calculating the female/male ratio of the "apparent enrolment rates" for each grade/form, for primary and for secondary school. Why do these ratios differ slightly from the female/male ratios of the numbers enrolled?
_____
_____
_____

3. Finish plotting these "apparent enrolment rates" separately for each sex on exercise figure 4. On the same graph plot the female/male ratio of these "rates". At which primary grade(s) are girls at greatest relative

disadvantage? _____ At which secondary form(s)? _____

4. Discuss the differences in school enrolment patterns of boys and girls. What are the policy implications suggested by these indicators, for all children? For girls in particular?
_____
_____
_____
_____
_____
_____
_____
_____

Exercise table 8. Apparent school enrolment, Zimbabwe, June 1979

	Population			School population and apparent enrolment rate							Percentage enrolment female	Female enrolment relative to male	
Age	Male	Female	Total		Male enrolment	Apparent rate	Female enrolment	Apparent rate	Total enrolment	Apparent rate		Female/male ratios Enrolment	Rate
7	118 760	115 376	234 136	Grade 1	87 067	73.3	83 058	72.0	170 125	72.7	48.8	95.4	98.2
8	113 392	110 416	223 808	Grade 2	72 532	64.0	67 476	61.1	140 008	62.6	48.2	93.0	95.5
9	108 409	105 030	213 439	Grade 3	70 777	65.3	59 393	56.1	130 170	60.7	45.6	83.9	85.9
10	103 812	101 609	205 421	Grade 4	57 848	55.7	51 829	51.0	109 677	53.4	47.3	89.6	91.6
11	99 595	97 738	197 333	Grade 5	53 241	53.5	45 560	46.6	98 801	50.1	46.1	85.6	----
12	95 443	93 997	189 440	Grade 6	49 073	51.4	39 355	41.9	88 428	46.7	44.5	80.2	----
13	91 195	90 201	181 396	Grade 7	47 147	51.7	35 230	39.1	82 377	45.4	42.8	74.7	----
Total 7-13	730 606	714 367	1 444 973	Total primary	437 685	59.9	381 901	53.4	819 586	56.7	46.6	87.3	----
14	86 955	86 475	173 430	Form I	9 804	11.3	8 645	10.0	18 449	10.7	46.9	88.2	----
15	82 979	82 993	165 972	Form II	8 823	10.6	7 315	8.8	16 138	9.7	45.3	82.9	----
16	79 206	79 715	158 921	Form III	7 750	9.8	5 975	7.5	13 725	8.7	43.5	77.1	----
17	75 614	76 531	152 145	Form IV	6 975	9.2	5 295	6.9	12 270	8.1	43.2	75.9	----
18	72 214	73 403	145 617	Form IV.L	2 625	3.6	1 936	2.6	4 561	3.1	42.4	73.8	----
19	68 987	70 358	139 345	Form IV.U	694	1.0	378	0.5	1 072	0.8	35.3	54.5	59.0
Total 14-19	465 955	469 475	935 430	Total secondary	36 671	7.9	29 544	6.3	66 215	7.1	44.6	80.6	----

Source: Data supplied by Zimbabwe Ministry of Education.

Exercise figure 4. Apparent enrolment rates, by class and sex, and female/male ratio, Zimbabwe, June 1979

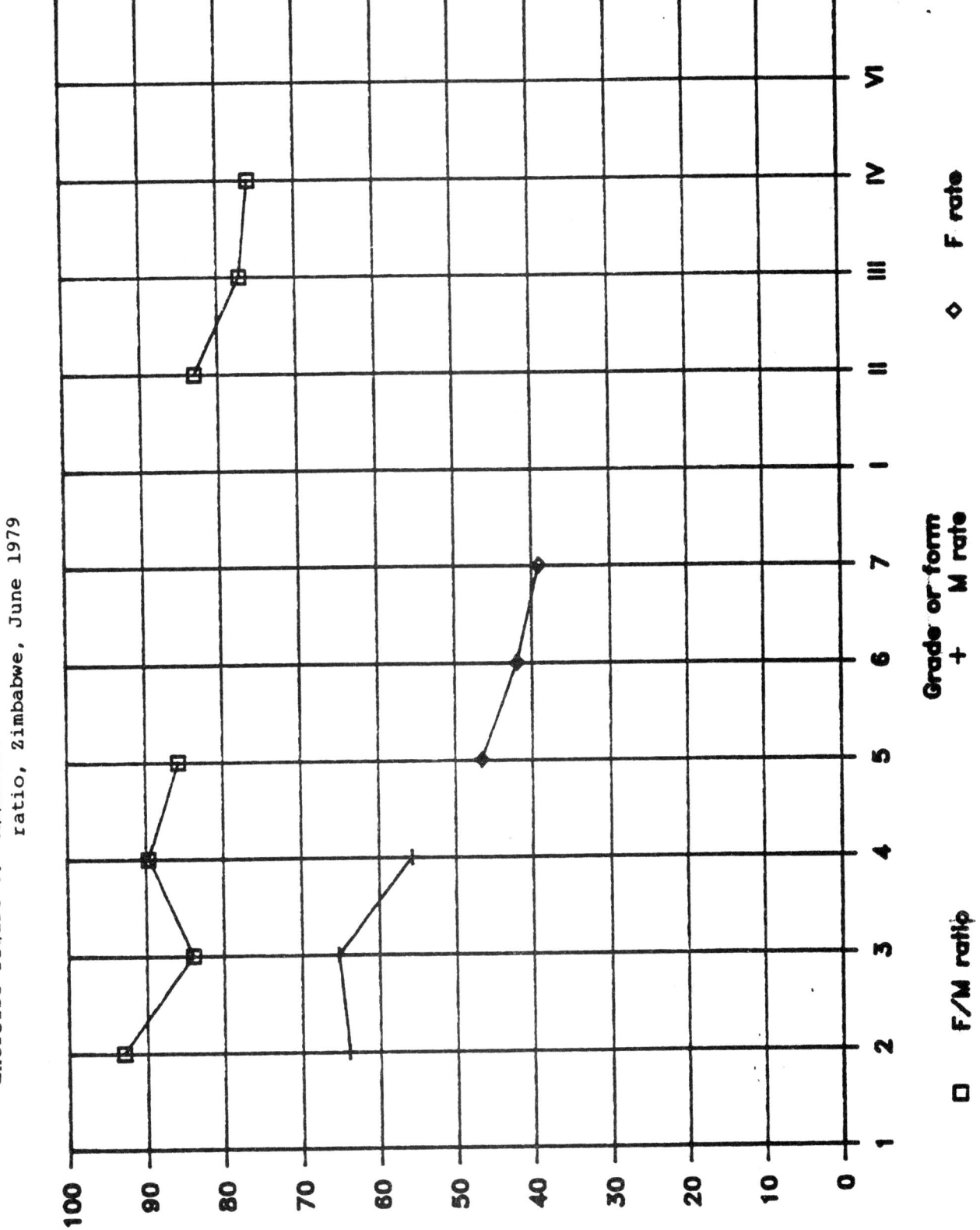

C. Enrolment in secondary and vocational/technical schools

When historical data are available we can monitor changes in women's access to non-vocational secondary schooling and to vocational/technical schooling over time.

1. Complete exercise table 9 by computing the percentage of non-vocational secondary students who were girls for each year, 1974 through 1983, in Botswana. For each column compute both absolute change and percentage change. What does this table suggest about the employment of women as secondary school teachers over the past decade? What does it suggest about the enrolment of girls in secondary schooling in Botswana? How does the educational situation of girls in Botswana compare with that in your own country?

_____
_____
_____

2. Compare exercise table 10 on enrolment in vocational/technical schools with table 9 on non-vocational secondary school enrolment. In what ways are the trends similar? In what ways different? What do you think these tables suggest about the preparation of women for employment in the modern sector? What are the policy implications of these data?

_____
_____
_____
_____

Exercise table 9. Teachers and students in government secondary schools (non-vocational), by sex and percentage female, Botswana, 1974-1983

	Teachers			Students		
Year	Male	Female	Percentage female	Male	Female	Percentage female
1974	244	106	30.3	3 654	3 481	48.2
1975	266	131	33.0	4 321	4 113	----
1976	297	148	33.4	4 744	4 814	----
1977	289	154	34.8	5 046	5 173	----
1978	317	188	37.2	5 400	5 736	----
1979	365	205	36.0	5 868	6 307	----
1980	397	237	37.4	6 420	7 004	----
1981	395	271	40.7	6 889	7 459	----
1982	..	..	..	7 066	7 434	----
1983	420	299	41.6	7 397	7 730	----
Change 1974-1983	----	----	11.3	----	----	----
Percentage change	----	----	37.3	----	----	----

Source: Data supplied by Botswana Ministry of Education, Education Statistics Unit.

Exercise table 10. Teachers and students in vocational and technical training, by sex and percentage female, Botswana, 1974-1981

	Teachers			Students		
Year	Male	Female	Percentage female	Male	Female	Percentage female
1974	141	48	25.3	906	622	40.7
1975	173	69	28.5	1 046	653	38.4
1976	152	64	29.6	1 023	699	40.6
1977	164	69	29.6	1 020	734	41.8
1978	265	75	22.1	1 082	508	31.9
1979	..	..	..	1 409	697	33.1
1980	125	102	44.9	1 349	451	25.1
1981	..	..	..	1 171	623	34.7
Change 1974-1980/81	-16	54	19.6	265	1	-6.0
Percentage change	-11.3	112.5	77.4	29.2	0.1	-14.7

Source: Data supplied by Botswana Ministry of Education, Education Statistics Unit.

D. Educational "tracking"

Even when girls are enrolled at secondary or higher levels, "tracking" tends to direct them into preparation for different (and often lower paying and lower prestige) occupations. In a world where technical skills are the key to participation in the modern sector, women will continue to be at a disadvantage if they have not had adequate training in such skills. Exercise tables 11-13 illustrates this tracking at each of three different kinds of institutions.

1. How might you use data like these for programme planning?

_____
_____
_____
_____

2. At what educational level do you think efforts should be concentrated to improve women's preparation for employment in the modern sector?

_____
_____
_____
_____
_____
_____
_____
_____

Exercise table 11. Number of fifth form science and art streams available, Kenya, 1976

Programme	Type of secondary school			
	Girls school	Boys school	Mixed	Total
Arts a/	26	28	12	66
Science b/	13	64	22	99
Total	39	92	34	165

Source: Kenya, Central Bureau of Statistics, Women in Kenya 1978 (Nairobi), p. 30.

a/ Arts streams average 35 places.

b/ Science streams average 30 places.

Exercise table 12. Vocational school enrolment, by course and sex, Botswana, 1983

Trades	Female	Male	Total	Percentage female
Industrial, mechanical	53	1 848	1 901	2.9
Agricultural and farming	84	250	334	25.1
Health	483	92	575	84.0

Source: Data supplied by Botswana Ministry of Education, Education Statistics Unit.

Exercise table 13. Female post-graduate enrolment, by faculty, University of Nairobi, Kenya, 1976/77, 1977/78

Faculty	1976/77 Females Number	1976/77 Females Percentage	1977/78 Females Number	1977/78 Females Percentage
Agriculture	7	7	22	13
Architecture/Design	3	6	2	5
Arts	41	34	56	35
Commerce	1	4	3	8
Education	21	26	37	31
Engineering	-	-	-	-
Law	2	22	3	20
Medicine	6	12	11	16
Science	4	7	15	9
Veterinary medicine	4	19	4	21

Source: Kenya, Central Bureau of Statistics, Women in Kenya 1978 (Nairobi), p. 35.

Exercise III

ECONOMIC ACTIVITY

A. Deriving labour force indicators from questionnaires

At end of the present section, questionnaires are reproduced from surveys in Botswana and Ethiopia. Make a list for each country of the items on which information is collected. Prepare three dummy tables of high priority indicators which may be produced on the basis of the collected information.

B. Economic activity status

Exercise tables 14 and 15 are taken from 1981 census data for Botswana. They describe different aspects of the economic activity of women and men.

1. Examine both tables. Are the number of employees roughly comparable in the two tables?

---

2. Calculate for table 15 the participation rate for males and females in rural and urban areas. Analyse the difference in activity status between men and women and between urban and rural areas.

Exercise table 14. Estimated number of employees by sex and economic activity, Botswana, August 1983

	Male	Female	Total
Agriculture	3 870	648	4 518
Mining and quarrying	6 734	487	7 221
Manufacturing	7 593	2 203	9 796
Electricity and water	1 862	58	1 920
Construction	9 200	350	9 550
Commerce	9 024	6 231	15 255
Transport and communications	3 474	425	3 899
Finance and business services	4 346	1 609	5 955
Community and social services	2 178	1 328	3 506
Education	706	859	1 565
Subtotal (private and parastatal)	48 987	14 198	63 185
Central government	18 700	11 400	30 100
Local government	5 039	2 169	7 208
Total	72 726	27 767	100 493

Source: Data compiled from Botswana Central Statistical Office, Employment Survey, 1983.

Exercise table 15. Type of economic activity, population aged 15-64 years, by sex and urban/rural residence

Economic activity status	Urban Males	Urban Females	Rural Males	Rural Females	Total Males	Total Females
Employee	39 986	17 957	41 062	8 787	81 048	26 744
Self-employed	1 679	1 205	3 349	2 080	5 028	3 285
Periodic piece-work	472	214	3 371	1 718	3 843	1 932
Family agriculture	961	2 343	58 592	54 684	59 553	57 027
Actively looking for work	4 251	5 280	9 662	11 573	13 913	16 853
Economically inactive	10 048	23 754	24 502	104 857	34 550	128 611
Total	57 397	50 753	140 538	183 699	197 935	234 452

Source: Data compiled from Botswana 1981 population census.

C. Presenting economic indicators

Exercise figure 5 and exercise table 16 show two ways of presenting the number of employees by sex and occupation.

1. Discuss the advantages and disadvantages of each presentation.

---

2. Select five occupations from the Kenya figures and construct bar diagrams separately for the employment of men and women in the public and private sectors.

Exercise table 16. Sex distribution of wage employment by occupational group and sector, Kenya, 1976

Occupational group	Public Males	Public Females	Private Males	Private Females
Casual employees	25 937	3 336	62 965	26 176
Unskilled workers	120 932	11 574	232 777	35 518
Skilled manual workers	31 376	5 153	49 632	1 966
Technicians and supervisors	6 180	255	5 758	325
Shop assistants, sales personnel	253	40	5 114	38
Clerical workers	26 262	2 480	18 504	2 078
Secretarial workers	450	5 108	730	4 771
Middle level executives	6 944	641	7 201	473
General managers	885	14	2 293	88
Teachers	63 464	32 123	2 157	654
Architects, engineers, and surveyors	894	5	488	9
Medical, dental, veterinary	1 646	1 523	117	144
Agronomists	330	21	37	0
Statisticians and mathematicians	126	6	50	16
Other scientists	341	28	47	3
Lawyers and jurists	139	9	39	7
Accountants	248	7	374	18
Economists	67	1	8	0
Other professions	1 789	109	1 754	226
Total	288 263	62 433	390 045	72 510

Source: Kenya, Ministry of Finance and Planning, Central Bureau of Statistics, Women in Kenya, 1978, based on the Labour Enumeration Survey, 1976.

Exercise figure 5. The 20 most popular occupations in Sweden, 1980, listed by size, percentage each sex

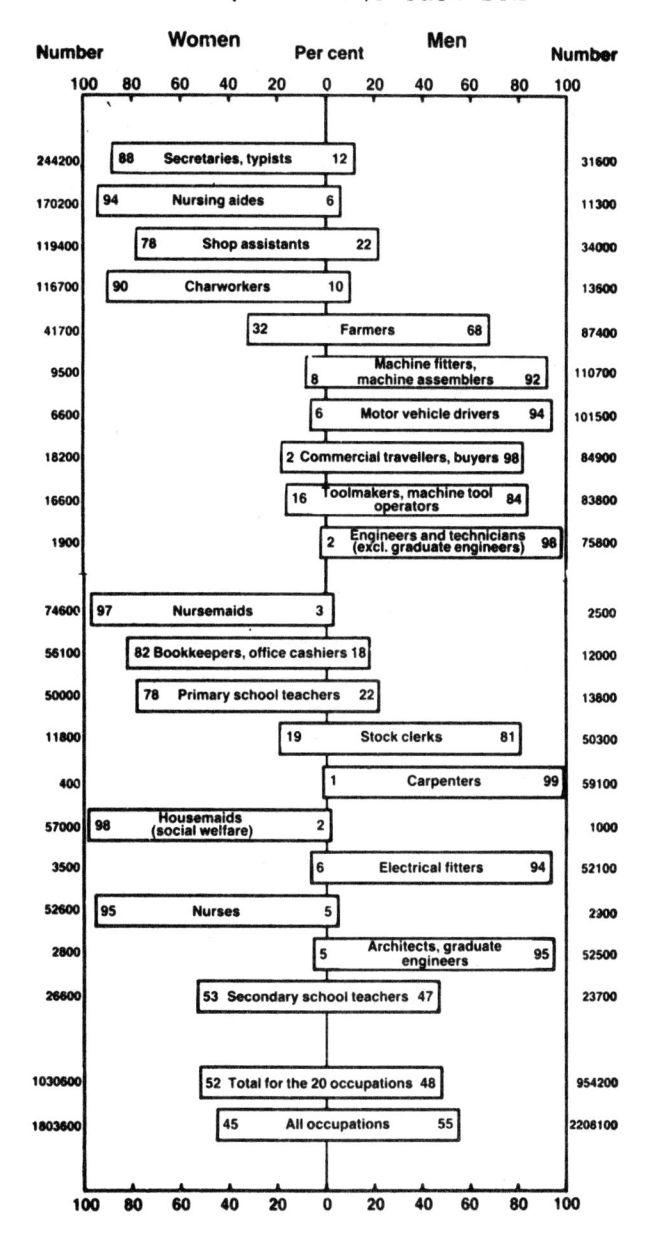

Women Number	Women %	Occupation	Men %	Men Number
244200	88	Secretaries, typists	12	31600
170200	94	Nursing aides	6	11300
119400	78	Shop assistants	22	34000
116700	90	Charworkers	10	13600
41700	32	Farmers	68	87400
9500	8	Machine fitters, machine assemblers	92	110700
6600	6	Motor vehicle drivers	94	101500
18200	2	Commercial travellers, buyers	98	84900
16600	16	Toolmakers, machine tool operators	84	83800
1900	2	Engineers and technicians (excl. graduate engineers)	98	75800
74600	97	Nursemaids	3	2500
56100	82	Bookkeepers, office cashiers	18	12000
50000	78	Primary school teachers	22	13800
11800	19	Stock clerks	81	50300
400	1	Carpenters	99	59100
57000	98	Housemaids (social welfare)	2	1000
3500	6	Electrical fitters	94	52100
52600	95	Nurses	5	2300
2800	5	Architects, graduate engineers	95	52500
26600	53	Secondary school teachers	47	23700
1030600	52	Total for the 20 occupations	48	954200
1803600	45	All occupations	55	2208100

Source: Statistics Sweden, <u>Women and Men in Sweden</u> (Stockholm, 1985) pp. 38-39.

Note: Half of all those gainfully employed worked in the 20 most popular occupations in 1980 - 60 per cent of all women and 40 per cent of all men. The nine most popular occupations among men are included in these. The tenth most popular occupation for women is kitchen assistant (44,600 women and 4,100 men).

Exercise tables 17 and 18 provide information on the economically active population in rural Ethiopia in 1970.

1. Which are the most important items of information in these tables?

2. What indicators of women's economic activity may be derived from this information?

3. What do you think might be an effective way of presenting these indicators?

Exercise table 17. Total rural population, population aged 10 years and over and economically active population, by sex (thousands), Ethiopia

	Males	Females	Total
Total population	11 245.6	10 781.4	22 027.0
Population aged 10+	7 523.2	7 105.2	14 628.4
Size of labour force	7 034.2	2 337.6	9 371.8
Participation rate (percentage)	93.5	32.9	64.1

Source: Ethiopia, Central Statistical Office, Tables of Demographic Data, vol. II, parts 1 and 2 (1978) and The Demography of Ethiopia (1974).

Exercise table 18. Percentage distribution of economically active population by status, sex and region, rural areas, Ethiopia, 1970

Region	Employer Males	Employer Females	Own-account worker Males	Own-account worker Females	Employee Males	Employee Females	Unpaid family worker Males	Unpaid family worker Females	Others economically active Males	Others economically active Females	Total Males	Total Females
Arssi	2.7	0.6	56.9	13.3	4.6	2.2	35.8	83.4	----	----	100.0	100.0
Bale	1.0	0.3	64.1	17.9	2.4	1.1	32.5	80.7	----	----	100.0	100.0
Eritrea	..	..	..	..	..	..	..	..	..	..	..	..
Gamo Gofa	0.3	0.2	70.2	24.6	1.7	3.5	27.8	71.6	----	----	100.0	100.0
Gojjam	1.4	0.1	56.0	14.2	5.5	4.8	36.8	80.9	0.3	----	100.0	100.0
Gonder	4.3	0.6	48.3	18.4	6.2	9.3	41.2	71.7	--	----	100.0	100.0
Hararge	0.7	..	64.7	27.4	2.0	41.9	32.6	30.7	----	----	100.0	100.0
Illubabor	0.8	0.2	74.5	6.4	1.8	0.5	22.8	92.9	0.1	----	100.0	100.0
Kefa	1.1	0.5	69.8	9.4	3.0	2.4	26.1	87.7	----	----	100.0	100.0
Shewa	2.6	0.2	56.9	10.5	5.4	3.2	35.1	86.1	----	----	100.0	100.0
Sidamo	0.2	0.8	68.5	65.7	0.9	3.2	30.4	29.9	0.2	0.4	100.0	100.0
Tigrai	2.8	0.5	49.1	21.8	7.6	13.7	39.7	62.4	0.8	1.6	100.0	100.0
Wollega	1.6	..	60.6	7.2	4.3	1.8	33.5	91.0	----	----	100.0	100.0
Wollo	3.7	1.1	52.4	19.8	8.0	16.5	35.5	62.5	0.4	0.1	100.0	100.0
Total	2.1	0.4	58.8	13.4	4.7	5.1	34.4	81.1	1.8	2.1	100.0	100.0

Source: Ethiopia, Central Statistical Office, Tables of Demographic Data, vol. II, parts 1 and 2 (1974) and The Demography of Ethiopia (1974).

Exercise IV

HEALTH STATUS, HEALTH SERVICES AND NUTRITION

A. Mortality by age and sex

Exercise tables 19 and 20 present data from Botswana for 1981. Table 19 shows the composition of the population by age and sex. Table 20 shows numbers of deaths and the death rates using these same age group and sex group classifications, as well as three indicators comparing female and male deaths: percentage female, female/male ratio of deaths, and female/male ratio of death rates.

1. Complete table 20, calculating the three indicators. Which of the three indicators do you think would be most useful in helping a health planner identify those ages of special vulnerability for girls and women relative to men? For boys and men relative to women?

2. Exercise figure 6 shows female/male ratios of death rates by age group, using data from table 20 for ages 0-44. Plot the female/male ratios for ages 45 and over onto the same graph. Which line do you think provides a better visual description of the female risk of dying relative to the male by age? In what age group are males at greatest risk relative to females?

-113-

Exercise table 19. Population by sex and age group, Botswana, 1981

Age group	Female	Male	Total
0	21 289	21 413	42 702
1-2	29 458	29 418	58 876
3-4	35 337	35 238	70 575
5-9	74 653	74 301	148 954
10-14	61 018	58 709	119 727
15-19	49 485	42 972	92 457
20-24	45 739	32 646	78 385
25-29	36 075	26 498	62 573
30-34	25 817	20 327	46 144
35-39	20 618	16 826	37 444
40-44	18 089	15 600	33 689
45-49	15 642	13 575	29 217
50-54	12 792	11 424	24 216
55-59	11 827	10 090	21 917
60-64	8 644	8 477	17 121
65+	31 440	25 590	57 030
Total	497 923	443 104	941 027

Source: Data compiled from Botswana 1981 population census.

Exercise table 20. Deaths and death rates per 1,000 population, by sex and age group: percentage female, female/male ratios of deaths and death rates, Botswana

Age group 1	Female Number 2	Female Rate 3	Male Number 4	Male Rate 5	Total 6 (2+4)	Percentage female 7 (2/6)*100	Female/male ratios of deaths 8 (2/4)	Female/male ratios of rates 9 (3/5)
0	1 136	53.4	1 415	66.1	2 551	44.5	0.803	0.808
1-2	453	15.4	544	18.5	997	45.4	0.833	0.832
3-4	229	6.5	254	7.2	483	47.4	0.902	0.903
1-4	(682)	(10.5)	(798)	(12.3)	(1 480)	(46.1)	(0.855)	(0.854)
5-9	209	2.8	219	2.9	428	48.8	0.954	0.966
10-14	128	2.1	166	2.8	294	43.5	0.771	0.750
5-14	(337)	(2.5)	(385)	(2.9)	(722)	(46.7)	(0.875)	(0.862)
15-19	124	2.5	138	3.2	262	47.3	0.899	0.781
20-24	162	3.5	202	6.2	364	44.5	0.802	0.565
15-24	(286)	(3.0)	(340)	(4.5)	(626)	(45.7)	(0.841)	(0.667)
25-29	147	4.1	236	8.9	383	38.4	0.623	0.461
30-34	133	5.2	213	10.5	346	38.4	0.624	0.495
35-39	134	6.5	175	10.4	309	43.4	0.766	0.625
40-44	103	5.7	193	12.4	296	34.8	0.534	0.460
25-44	(517)	(5.1)	(817)	(10.3)	(1 334)	(38.8)	(0.633)	(0.495)
45-49	120	----	189	----	309	----	----	----
50-54	122	----	194	----	316	----	----	----
55-59	141	----	183	----	324	----	----	----
45-59	(383)	(9.5)	(566)	(16.1)	(949)	(40.4)	(0.677)	(0.590)
60-64	113	----	224	----	337	----	----	----
65+	960	----	1 229	----	2 189	----	----	----
60+	(1 073)	(26.8)	(1 453)	(42.7)	(2 526)	(42.5)	(0.738)	(0.628)
Total	4 414	----	5 774	----	10 188	----	----	----

Source: Botswana 1981 population census.

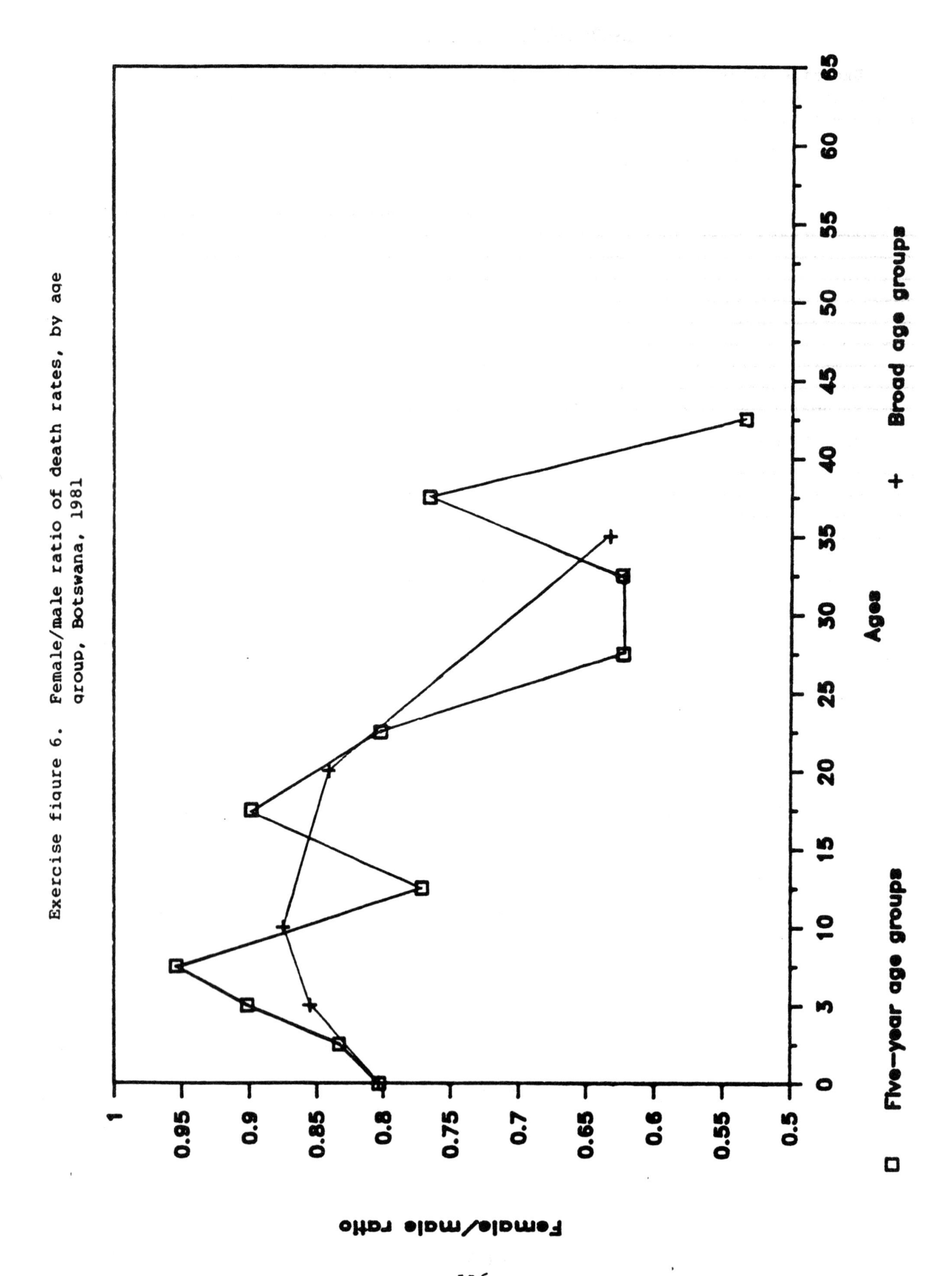

Exercise figure 6. Female/male ratio of death rates, by age group, Botswana, 1981

B. Infant mortality and child survival

Exercise table 21 presents mortality rates and percentage of children dying before their fifth birthday for several countries in sub-Saharan Africa for which reliable estimates are available.

1. Complete the table, calculating female/male ratios for each indicator. Which ratio would you expect to show greater variability? Why?

_____
_____
_____
_____
_____
_____
_____
_____
_____
_____
_____

2. Calculate the medians for each of the six indicators.

_____
_____
_____
_____
_____

Exercise table 21. Infant mortality and child survival

Country	Year	Infant mortality rates Female	Male	Female/male ratio	Percentage of children dying before their fifth birthday Female	Male	Female/male ratio
EASTERN AFRICA							
Burundi	1970-71	132	147	0.90	26.5	27.4	0.97
Kenya	1977	78	87	0.90	13.3	15.4	0.86
Mauritius	1980	31	35	0.89	..	..	..
Rwanda	1977	120	135	0.89	24.2	27.4	----
Seychelles a/	1975	28	32	0.88	4.9	5.2	----
Somalia b/	1974-78	144	176	----	..	..	..
Uganda	1969	111	129	----	19.1	21.2	----
SOUTHERN AFRICA							
Botswana	1964-71	91	103	----	13.9	16.6	----
Swaziland	1966-76	146	165	----	..	..	..
Median		----	----	----	----	----	----

Source: Data compiled from United States of America Bureau of the Census, Women in Development data base.

a/ Refers to averages of yearly rates: infant mortality 1975 to 1980, child mortality 1971 to 1975.

b/ Refers only to settled population in the Cenadir, Bay, Lower Shebelle areas.

C. Life expectancy at birth by sex

Exercise table 22 presents life expectancies at birth and female/male ratios of life expectancy for a number of countries in sub-Saharan Africa.

1. Complete the column giving female/male ratios.

2. Identify those countries with an estimate dated between 1965 and 1974. What was the median expectation of life in 1970 for countries for which such estimates are available?

Exercise table 22. Expectation of life at birth for women and men
and female/male ratio of life expectancies

Country	Year	Women	Men	Female/male ratio
Western Africa				
The Gambia	1973	34.3	32.2	1.07
Ghana	1970	50.2	46.9	1.07
Liberia	1970-71	48.6	45.6	1.07
Mali	1960-61	35.7	33.7	1.06
Mauritania a/	1965	36.0	32.0	1.13
Niger	1960	40.1	37.0	1.08
Nigeria	1971-73	43.0	39.5	1.09
Senegal	1970-71	44.2	43.0	1.03
Sierra Leone	1974	35.9	33.0	1.09
Togo	1961	42.7	41.8	1.02
Burkina Faso b/	1960-61	31.9	33.0	0.97
Central Africa				
Cameroon	1976	45.5	43.1	1.06
Chad	1964	35.0	29.0	1.21
Eastern Africa				
Burundi	1970-71	43.1	40.5	----
Kenya	1977	55.8	51.2	----
Mauritius	1971-73	65.3	60.7	----
Rwanda	1970	42.0	38.0	----
Seychelles	1974-&8	71.1	64.6	----
Uganda	1969	46.9	45.8	----
Zambia	1969	46.5 c/	43.0 d/	----
Southern Africa				
Botswana	1964-71	58.3	52.3	----
Swaziland	1966-76	49.5	42.9	----

Source: Data compiled from United Sates of America, Bureau of the Census, Women in Development data base.

a/ Rural area only.

b/ Rural and semi-urban.

c/ Range: 45.0-47.5.

d/ Range: 41.8-44.3.

D. Nutritional status

1. Part A of exercise table 23 shows numbers and percentage distributions of rural Kenyan children under age 5 by two different measures of nutritional status: weight-for-height and height-for-age. Weight-for-height responds fairly rapidly to short-term calorie deprivation while height-for-age is a longer-term measure of chronic undernutrition. Would you expect to see a relationship between these two measures in a population of children? Does such a relationship appear in these data? Do you think both indicators are needed to describe nutritional status adequately? What is an important common limitation?

_____
_____
_____
_____
_____

2. The upper panel of part B of table 23 shows the nutritional status of the same population of children by age. At what age do you think children are at greatest risk of serious illness or death due to malnutrition, as an underlying if not the major cause?

_____
_____
_____
_____
_____

3. The lower panel of part B of table 23 shows nutritional status by sex. Complete the table by calculating the female/male ratio for each nutritional status. What can you say about the relative nutritional status of girls and boys under age 5 in this population? Data are not available by sex and age combined; however, if you assume that the female/male ratio of nutritional status is similar for all ages under 5, which age and sex group of children is at highest risk? Excluding infant mortality, much of which is due to other causes, are these data consistent with the age and sex distribution of mortality in health status exercise A?

_____
_____
_____

Exercise table 23. Nutritional status

A. Children under 5 years by weight-for-height and height-for-age

Weight-for-height	Height-for-age							
	100 per cent of standard		99-90 per cent (marginally stunted)		less than 90 percent (stunted)		Total	
	Number	Per cent	Number	Per cent	Number	Per cent	Number	Per cent
>90 per cent of standard (normal)	675	12.7	2 632	49.5	1 083	20.3	4 390	82.5
90-80 per cent (marginally wasted)	164	3.1	438	8.2	170	3.2	772	14.5
<80 per cent (wasted)	59	1.1	77	1.4	24	0.5	160	3.0
Total	898	16.9	3 147	59.1	1 277	24.0	5 322	100.0

B. Percentage distribution of children by nutritional status, by age and sex.

	Nutritional status			
	Total	Normal	Stunted only	Wasted only	Stunted and wasted
Age (months)					
3-11	100.0	75.2	22.3	2.3	0.1
12-23	100.0	51.6	38.2	7.3	2.9
24-35	100.0	48.2	48.1	2.7	1.1
36-47	100.0	59.7	37.7	2.1	0.4
48-60	100.0	62.2	34.0	2.9	0.9
Female	100.0	60.1	36.6	3.3	0.9
Male	100.0	56.8	38.2	3.6	1.3
Female/male ratio	----	----	----	----	----

Source: Kenya, Central Bureau of Statistics, Third Rural Child Nutritional Survey, 1982 (Nairobi, 1983), p. 79.

E. National health services availability

Exercise table 24 presents data on the numbers of physicians, nurses and midwives, and hospital facilities and beds for countries of eastern and southern Africa. In exercise table 25, national-level indicators of health services availability are given, computed from table 24.

1. Complete table 25, calculating indicators of availability of nurses/midwives and beds.

2. Compute medians for each of the six indicators of table 25, for the countries of eastern and southern Africa:

	Population per physician	Physicians per 10,000 population	Population per nurse	Nurses per 10,000 population	Population per bed	Beds per 10,000 population
Median:	_____	_____	2,300	_____	_____	_____

3. Which country has the highest number of physicians per 10,000 population? _____ The lowest? _____

4. Do these countries also rank among the five highest and five lowest in nurses per population? _____ In beds per population? _____

5. What do you conclude about the availability of medical resources in the region? In your country relative to the region?

_____
_____
_____
_____
_____
_____
_____
_____

-123-

Exercise table 24. Health services statistics

Geographical area	Population (000s)	Physicians	Nurses/midwives Qualified	Nurses/midwives Assistants	Facilities with beds Establishments	Facilities with beds Beds
World	4 134 667	3 342 587	5 708 025	1 856 877	..	..
Africa a/	394 457	64 890	133 583	118 106	..	..
Northern	99 846	46 417	35 431	57 939	..	..
Western	122 532	8 188	59 889	20 282	..	..
Central	49 745	3 233	9 759	21 413	..	..
Eastern	119 897	6 859	27 242	17 957	..	..
Burundi	3 680	81	262	417	136	4 221
Comoros	291	19	86	79	30	612
Djibouti	111	64	158	115	11	1 050
Ethiopia	28 925	396	1 488	..	84	8 746
Kenya	14 500	1 270	1 320	4 250	65	17 896
Madagascar	8 520	784	825	2 668	891	19 962
Malawi	5 526	116	397	1 040	324	9 617
Mauritius	909	376	1 586	173	35	3 220
Mozambique	9 678	285	2 006	372	588	11 041
Reunion	480	304	1 133	598	11	2 642
Rwanda	4 455	120	389	516	201	7 162
Seychelles	58	21	124	10	7	300
Somalia	3 003	193	998	..	..	5 163
Tanzania	15 985	1 003	5 875	1 794	2 422	34 589
Uganda	12 350	436	1 197	3 982	420	18 156
Zambia	4 896	472	2 490	..	758	20 030
Zimbabwe	6 530	919	6 908	1 943	..	17 393
Southern	2 437	193	1 262	515	..	..
Botswana	690	72	277	267	21	2 137
Lesotho	1 250	67	295	38	88	2 564
Swaziland	497	54	690	210	33	1 717

Source: World Health Organization, World Health Statistics Annual; Health Personnel and Hospital Establishments (Geneva, 1980). Data relate to various years in the period 1973 to 1978.

a/ South Africa not included.

Exercise table 25. Health services indicators

Geographical area	Population per physician	Physicians per 10,000 population	Population per nurse/mid-wife	Nurses/mid-wives per 10,000 population	Population per bed	Beds per 10,000 population
World	1 237	8.08	547	18.30	..	..
Africa a/	6 079	1.65	1 567	6.38	..	..
Northern	2 151	4.65	1 069	9.35	..	..
Western	14 965	0.67	1 528	6.54	..	..
Central	15 387	0.65	1 596	6.27	..	..
Eastern	17 480	0.57	2 653	3.77	..	..
Burundi	45 432	0.22	5 420	1.85	872	11.47
Comoros	15 316	0.65	1 764	5.67	475	21.03
Djibouti	1 734	5.77	407	24.59	106	94.59
Ethiopia	73 043	0.14	19 439 b/	0.51 b/	3 307	3.02
Kenya	11 417	0.88	2 603	3.84	810	12.34
Madagascar	10 867	0.92	2 439	4.10	427	23.43
Malawi	47 638	0.21	3 846	2.60	575	17.40
Mauritius	2 418	4.14	517	19.35	282	35.42
Mozambique	33 958	0.29	4 070	2.46	877	11.41
Reunion	1 579	6.33	277	36.06	182	55.04
Rwanda	37 125	0.27	4 923	2.03	622	16.08
Seychelles	2 762	3.62	433	23.10	193	51.72
Somalia	15 560	0.64	3 009 b/	3.32 b/	582	17.19
Tanzania	15 937	0.63	2 084	4.80	----	----
Uganda	28 326	0.35	2 385	4.19	----	----
Zambia	10 373	0.96	1 966 b/	5.90 b/	----	----
Zimbabwe	7 106	1.41	738	13.55	----	----
Southern	12 627	0.79	1 371	7.29	..	..
Botswana	9 583	1.04	----	----	----	----
Lesotho	18 657	0.54	----	----	----	----
Swaziland	9 204	1.09	----	----	----	----

Source: Data calculated from table 24.

a/ South Africa not included.

b/ Qualified only.

F. Women's utilization of health services

1. The statistics below are based on exercise table 26. Which are appropriate indicators of women's utilization of health services?

_____
_____
_____
_____

2. What do they suggest for programme priorities?

_____
_____
_____
_____

Botswana, second quarter, 1984

Population	1,013,382	Children under 5	185,387
Total visits	451,326	First well-child visits	8,512
Visits per person	0.45	Repeat well-child visits	365,601
- Per person per year	1.78	Total well-child visits	374,113
Women, 15-49	227,186 a/		
Estimated births	11,944 b/	Ratio: first well-child visits to total well-child visits	0.02
First ante-natal visits	7,185		
Ratio: first ante-natal visits to estimated births	0.60	Ratio: total well-child visits to all children 5	2.02
Post-natal visits	3,312	- per year	8.07
Ratio: post-natal to first ante-natal visits	0.46	Ratio: first well-child visit to estimated births	0.71

a/ Projected from 1981 to 1984 at an annual growth rate of 2.5 per cent.

b/ Number of live births per 1,000 women aged 15-49 in Botswana per year estimated at 210.3. Estimated live births in the second quarter 1984 thus equals (210.3/4) x (227,186/1,000) = 11,944.

Exercise table 26. Out-patient and preventive health services, Botswana, second quarter, 1984

Facility type	Number of visits	Injections and dressings	Family planning	Ante-natal care New	Ante-natal care Repeat	Post-natal care	Well-child care New	Well-child care Repeat
Hospitals	118 548	93 146	3 933	1 557	9 645	706	774	13 572
Health centres	22 795	14 747	1 494	335	2 381	252	356	16 815
Clinics	218 293	165 232	23 571	3 708	23 986	1 977	4 951	199 256
Health posts	91 726	36 540	6 721	1 585	7 704	377	2 431	135 958
Total	451 362	309 665	35 719	7 185	43 716	3 312	8 512	365 601

Annex I

OPENING AND CLOSING STATEMENTS

At the opening session, the Honourable Teurai Ropa Nhongo, Minister of Community Development and Women's Affairs, Zimbabwe, introduced the theme of the Seminar. He stated that in developing strategies for effective utilization of the nation's human resources, it was essential to have complete and accurate information on women's contribution to national growth and development, on the impediments to their full participation in such development, and on the impact of development in turn upon women. Although data on the situation of women were often inadequate, the problem was not always lack of data <u>per se</u>. To develop appropriate human resource policies and plans, those data must be translated into meaningful statistics and indicators. By improving the abililty of countries to produce and make use of such statistics and indicators, the Seminar would have an impact not only on the participation of women in development but also on the pace of development itself.

The representatives of the United Nations Development Programme and United Nations Fund for Population Activities reiterated the support of the United Nations system for women and development activities, stressing that the participation of women in development was a matter of economic necessity, not simply one of distributive justice. The representatives of the International Research and Training Institute for the Advancement of Women and the Economic Commission for Africa/African Training and Research Centre for Women described the hopes and objectives of the organizers in holding the Seminar.

Gibson Mandishona, Director of the Central Statistical Office of Zimbabwe reminded participants that indicators were policy-relevant statistics which served as broad guidelines and showed whether a nation was retreating or progressing towards its multiple objectives. Mr. Mandishona called for the development of an adequate conceptual framework to guide the preparation and use of statistics and indicators for national development, suggesting the compilation of five groups of indicators on both women and men: basic needs, popular participation in national life, national security, economic performance and population phenomena.

At the close of the Seminar, following remarks made by the representatives of the sponsoring organizations, Angela Makwavarara (Ministry of Community Development and Women's Affairs, Zimbabwe) congratulated the participants and organizers of the Seminar for bringing the issues discussed to the attention of policy-makers and the public. She urged participants to keep each other informed about their efforts and achievements in improving information on women. Speaking for the Minister of Economic Development of Zimbabwe, Mr. Mandishona reviewed the accomplishments of the Seminar and pointed to gaps in information and priority areas for further work. The central statistical offices played a critical role but their resources were limited. Others needed to supplement the activities of those offices in developing information about women for planning and monitoring policies and programmes. Mr. Mandishona suggested a series of national follow-up seminars and noted that Zimbabwe was now planning to hold such a seminar in 1986.

Annex II

LIST OF PARTICIPANTS

National delegations

BOTSWANA

Ms. Gwen Ntenda Lesetedi
Central Statistics Office

Mrs. N. Mbere
Applied Research Unit
Ministry of Local Government and
  Lands

Ms. Godisang B. Mookodi
Women's Affairs Unit
Ministry of Home Affairs

ETHIOPIA

Ms. Abaynesh Makonnen
Central Statistics Office

Ms. Kelemework Tekle
Coffee Marketing Corporation

Ms. Hirut Terefe
Addis Ababa University

Ms. Elsa Teferi
Office of the National Committee
  for Central Planning

KENYA

Mr. D. O. Ahawo
Central Bureau of Statistics

Ms. Mary Mbeo
Women's Bureau

Ms. Gladys Mulindi
Maendeleo ya Wanaweka

LESOTHO

Mr. Francis M. Hloaele
Department of Youth and Women's
  Affairs
Prime Minister's Office

MADAGASCAR

Mr. James R. Ravelojoana
Ministry of Population and Social
  Condition

MALAWI

Mr. F. S. Chatsalira
Ministry of Community Services

Mr. William H. Mbale
Social Statistics Section
National Statistics Office

MAURITIUS

Mr. Harish Bundhoo
Central Statistical Office

SOMALIA

Ms. Sahara Aden Diriye
Planning Section
Somalia Women's Democratic
  Organization

Mr. Awil Mohamed Farah
Central Statistics Office

UGANDA

Ms. Margaret H. Odwongo
Ministry of Culture and Community
  Development

UNITED REPUBLIC OF TANZANIA

Ms. Elizabeth Maro Minde
Co-operative College

Mr. Cletus P. B. Mkai
Bureau of Statistics

ZAMBIA

Ms. Dorothy Kapantha
United Independence Party (UNIP)

Ms. Celestina L. C. Ssewankambo
Central Statistics Office

Ms. Susan Sikaneta Yoyo
Research Bureau, UNIP

ZIMBABWE

Central Statistical Office:

Mr. Gibson Mandishona
Mr. J. Z. Mzelethi
Mr. David J. Mzite
Ms. Joyce Ndudzo
Mr. Rodwell K. Shumha
Mr. R. Tendere

Mr. Zaipa Herbert Chigwada
Department of the Registrar-General

Mr. S. E. Chikwana
Ministry of Health

Mr. Samson D. Gumbo
Ministry of Education

Ms. Ia Phylis Mafethe
Rural Health Services
Ministry of Health

ZIMBABWE (continued)

Ms. Margaret Mwalo
Ministry of Labour, Manpower,
   Planning and Social Welfare

Mrs. Munyikwa
Ministry of Community Development
   and Women's Affairs

Ms. R. L. Nkomo
Ministry of Lands Resettlement and
   Rural Development

Ms. Usha Patel
Training and Research
Ministry of Construction and National
   Housing

Mr. Paul S. S. Shumba
Zimbabwe National Family Council

Mr. W. N. Tichagwa
Ministry of Community Development and
   Women's Affairs

Ms. Kate Truscott
Ministry of Agriculture

Mr. Naison Zumbika
Agricultural Finance Corporation

Observers

Canadian International Development Agency: Mr. Stephen Wallace

Food and Agricultural Organization of the United Nations: Mr. D. C. Alonzo

United Nations Children's Fund:

   Mr. R. Decoster, Mrs. Hapte-Mariam and Mrs. S. Haji-Ahmed

United Nations Development Programme: Ms. Birgit Madsen

United Nations Fund for Population Activities: Ms. Tisitsi Nheta

Eastern and Southern Africa Management Institute, Arusha, Tanzania:
Ms. Misrak Elias

Zimbabwe

Central Statistical Office: Mr. R. Tendere, Ms. Sabina T. Banda, Mr. Rodwell K. Shumba

Ministry of Community Development and Women's Affairs: Mrs. Mena Mujnyikwa

Ministry of Health: Mr. R. Shiraz

University of Zimbabwe: Prof. Robert Mazur

Organizers

United Nations Economic Commission for Africa (ECA)

    African Training and Research Centre for Women (ECA/ATRCW):

        Ms. Nancy J. Hafkin

        Ms. Mekdes Gabre Medhin

    Statistics Division:

        Mr. Toma John Makannah

Multinational Programming and Operational Centre (MULPOC), Lusaka, Zambia:

    Mr. Kuezi-Nke

International Training and Research Institute for the Advancement of Women:

    Ms. Mervat Tallawy

    Ms. Jeanne S. Newman, Technical Co-ordinator (Consultant)

Statistical Office, Department of International Economic and Social Affairs, United Nations Secretariat:

    Ms. Joann Vanek

    Ms. Grace Bediako (Consultant)

Annex III

AIDE MEMOIRE

A. Organization

The Subregional Seminar on Improved Statistics and Indicators for Women in Development, sponsored by the Economic Commission for Africa and the International Research and Training Institute for the Advancement of Women in co-operation with the Statistical Office of the United Nations Secretariat, is being held in Harare, Zimbabwe, from 29 April through 7 May 1985. It will be hosted by the Government of Zimbabwe through the Central Statistical Office and the Ministry of Community Development and Women's Affairs. Financial support has also come from the United Nations Fund for Population Activities and the United Nations Development Fund for Women.

The objectives of the Seminar are:

(a) To facilitate a dialogue between producers and users on the sources and application of statistics and indicators on women;

(b) To familiarize participants with:

   (i) Sources of data on women;

  (ii) The resources of national statistical offices;

 (iii) A variety of indicators useful for planning, monitoring and evaluating policies, plans and programmes for women in development, together with methods of calculation and presentation;

 (iv) Current and potential applications of these indicators and user organizations;

(c) To provide participants with experience in calculating and presenting a representative set of these indicators;

(d) To contribute to the ongoing search for better ways of incorporating data on women into national statistical series and of using such data in policy and programme planning, monitoring and evaluation.

The Seminar is the first of its kind, following up the INSTRAW/Statistical Office Expert Group Meeting on Improving Statistics and Indicators of the Situation of Women in Development (New York, 1983) as well as the ECA Subregional Seminar on the Utilization of Research by National Machineries for the Integration of Women in Development (Zimbabwe, 1982).

The programme will include lectures, panels, participatory discussions and programming exercises drawing on the INSTRAW/United Nations publication Compiling Social Indicators on the Situation of Women (which will be mailed to participants as soon as their nominations are received) and national materials on women and development gathered for this Seminar, with emphasis on practical possibilities for indicator compilation and application in each country. There will also be sessions on use of micro-computers for development and maintenance of data bases and for computings indicators.

B. Results expected

The Seminar is expected to result in follow-up work at the national level and increased communication at the national level between users and producers of statistics and indicators on women and development.

Participants have been invited from countries of the east and southern Africa subregion. Each delegation was requested to include a representative of the Central Statistical Office, preferably the official in charge of social statistics, and a representative of the national machinery for the integration of women in development, who should be working in a planning or research capacity.

The working language of the Seminar will be English. No translation or interpretation will be provided.

C. Programme

Among the topics included in the programme will be review of statistical concepts and methods for women and development planning related to statistics and indicators, demand for and applications of statistics and indicators for women and development planning, sources for statistics and indicators on women, assessment of relationships between national statistical services and users of their products, manipulation of statistics and indicators in specific fields, and promotion of national follow-up activities.

The Seminar will work in plenary as well as in small groups of 10 to 15 persons. The methods of work will include lectures, panels, participatory discussions, and exercises utilizing national data. Emphasis will be placed on stimulating communication between users and products of statistics. There will also be a one-day field trip to observe data collection sites of the African Household Capability Programme Survey as well as projects on women and development operated by the Ministry of Community Development and Women's Affairs.

Annex IV

FIELD VISITS

To provide participants with a more vivid sense of the problems and possibilities for data collection on women in rural areas and of the kinds of indicators needed by women's groups and those seeking to serve them, a one-day visit to Bindura, a rural community two hours outside Harare, was organized by the Central Statistical Office and the Ministry of Community Development and Women's Affairs.

A. Central Statistical Office field office, Bindura

During the morning the group met with field staff of the Central Statistical Office at the Bindura field office, where it learned about the structure and organization of the field offices and the data collection methods and schedule of the National Household Survey Programme. Presentations by four of the field staff were followed by questions and discussion.

A representative of the Economic Commission for Africa described the African Household Survey Capability Programme, in which Zimbabwe was participating. Under that programme, ECA assisted participating countries in organizing a permanent survey unit with the central statistical offices and regional field offices. Each country developed a five-year programme of topics to be investigated in accordance with national priorities covering, for example, labour force, agriculture, nutrition and population. Permanent staff of the survey unit planned all the surveys, supplemented by experts in the central statistical offices and the relevant ministries. Permanent trained enumerators and their supervisors helped to ensure competence and uniformity in survey implementation.

A provincial supervisor of the field office described the structure of the survey unit. At the centre in Harare was the head office. Each province had an office and was organized into eight districts, each with supervisors, team leaders and enumerators (four or five per team). Their task was to collect data on a continuing basis for ongoing statistical programmes, to formulate, implement and evaluate programmes in the provinces.

The sample design employed in these surveys was described. A master sampling frame, based on the August 1982 census, listed all households within specific economic/ecological areas: urban, commercial farming, peasant farming, and so on. The specific frame used depended upon the aim of the survey. Within each province, the population was divided into "Statistics Divisions" of 4,000 households. Divisions are selected by probability sampling, and within each Division two sections (of 200 households each) were selected systematically. The 200 households were listed by basic socio-economic and demographic characteristics and 10 were selected for interviewing by means of systematic sampling.

The process of survey implementation, using the recent 1984/85 survey of income, consumption and expenditures as a model, was also described. Finally, an enumerator team leader described some of the problems enumerators faced in the field. Maps and interview schedules must be prepared in the local languages; local authorities must be induced to publicize the survey locally or people would be reluctant to give information; randomly selected households must be reinterviewed to check for reliability; manual editing must be carried out daily to identify and solve problems in a timely fashion; confidentiality of responses must be ensured; accomodations for enumerators were inadequate in remote rural areas; transport must be secured; and so on.

During the discussion the following points were made:

(a) It was important not to overwork a sampled unit. Two years was the longest period that a household could remain in the sample;

(b) Enumerators must be retrained each year as survey topics changed;

(c) For some topics women enumerators might be better able to obtain information but the job was difficult for women. The population was widely dispersed and much of the work must be done at night. Safety was an issue, as was conflict with domestic responsibilities;

(d) Co-ordination between the Central Statistical Office and user ministries was achieved through an Inter-Ministerial Committee, chaired by the Director of the Central Statistical Office. More recently attempts had been made to involve parastatals;

(e) The appropriate respondent might not always be the "household head"; interviews with the "head" might not provide reliable information about others in the household who were not respondents.

B. Women's sewing group: a producers' pre-co-operative, Bindura

In the afternoon, participants visited the community centre to meet with a group of women who were seeking recognition from the Department of Co-operative Development as a producer's co-operative, to sew and market school uniforms.

To become a registered co-operative and thus eligible for a variety of assistance programmes, the group must demonstrate viability, that is, it must be profitable. It must buy new materials and build a savings account to build a factory or shop. The volume of business must grow and it must have a reasonable market. At present, the group was still too small to qualify, but it was working with the Ministry of Community Development and Women's Affairs to become viable and thus eligible for registration.

To become viable the group must solve a number of problems:

(a) Working capital, supplies and equipment: Each of the 24 initial members contributed $Z 10 for a total of $Z 240 of initial working capital, enough to purchase initial materials, but not to acquire the necessary sewing machines. They were now working with only two machines loaned by members. Those were insufficient and some members had dropped out because of this;

(b) Facilities: The Bindura Rural Council provided a place to work in the community centre, with water and electricity;

(c) Training:

    (i) Technical. The Ministry of Community Development and Women's Affairs had assisted in the cost of a two-week training course for the members - samples of school uniforms attested to the technical skill of the members;

    (ii) Management, administration, accounting. The group was greatly in need of assistance in these areas;

(d) Markets: There were six primary schools in the area. The group had set the price for a uniform at $8.00 and had given its output to local headmasters to sell. Some had been sold on credit. Assistance was needed to assess the potential market and to market the uniform.

Seminar participants had a number of questions and suggestions. They were concerned that appropriate channels be identified and mobilized to assist the women in acquiring the administrative and marketing skills and working capital needed to make their project viable. Moreover, participants had to identify the kinds of information the Ministry of Community Development and Women's Affairs and the Department of Co-operative Development would need to have in order to decide how to advise and help such a group. A representative of the Department of Co-operative Development agreed to assist the group in assessing its market. It was suggested that the Ministry of Community Development and Women's Affairs help to bring together several such groups and assist them in developing the information needed to prepare a proposal to the United Nations Development Fund for Women.

There was obvious frustration that a group of rural women who were technically skilled, ambitious and committed to their enterprise had found so little practical assistance in turning their efforts into a productive business.

The initial hour of the morning of the next day was devoted to a review and discussion of what had been observed on the field trip. The stark reality facing the sewing pre-co-operative group - loosely organized with only rudimentary literacy and great need for assistance - was the same reality facing thousands of such groups around the world. What kind of data collection about such groups could help the user organizations represented at the Seminar better plan to direct assistance to such groups?

In the discussion of the field trip, the following observations were made:

(a) On data collection and processing:

    (i) Could surveys be organized to obtain information from different members of the household? Survey research technology was progressing but it was costly to interview separate members of the household. Yet if present practice failed to yield adequate information, perhaps the methodology would need to be modified;

    (ii) Many central statistical offices had succeeded in planning and collecting data, only to be unable to process and disseminate the information sufficiently rapidly. The problem was magnified with a continuing data collection effort, as in Zimbabwe's Household Survey Programme. The solution might lie in decentralized data processing on microcomputers. Meanwhile, initial manual tabulations were published quickly and were reliable at the national and provincial levels. Users also collaborated by processing their own data and writing reports;

(b) On the needs of the women's sewing group:

    (i) In planning for assistance to women's groups, it was important to look at all beneficiaries, not just the participants but the community at large;

    (ii) Data currently being collected provided information on the number and variety of projects and on participants by project type but were not very helpful for monitoring and evaluation. Data on receipts and expenditures were unavailable;

    (iii) More information should be included in project proposals: on socio-economic background of participants, malnutrition, illiteracy in the community and so on. Perhaps the household survey programme could provide the needed statistical profiles at small area levels;

    (iv) Perhaps specific items could be added to the household survey questionnaire to obtain information on the kinds of changes introduced by women's projects;

    (v) Another possibility was to ask Provincial Community Development Offices to collect their own statistics, using agricultural extension workers to ask specific questions, separately of women and men;

    (vi) Women's groups needed to begin with a feasibility study to answer three questions:

        a. Are materials available?
        b. Is there a market?
        c. Can they obtain start-up funds?

    Can the provincial officers help them with such a feasibility study?

    (vii) Perhaps a very simple project proposal form could be developed for extension workers on which the needs of each group for technical assistance, equipment, and the like could be indicated. Those profiles of women's groups could then be brought together at the Ministry and used as a basis for developing and directing assistance to the groups.

Annex V

EVALUATION FORM

To participants:

Your response to the following questions will help us improve future seminars. On a 5-point scale (5 = very much, 1 = not at all), please assess the material and presentations in terms of usefulness to you. For each item, circle the rating which most accurately reflects your assessment and give us your comments or suggestions.

A. **Seminar design**

Please indicate how satisfied you were with each of the following:

		Very much				Not at all
1.	Overall design of the seminar	5	4	3	2	1
2.	Overall schedule	5	4	3	2	1
3.	Amount of time allocated for discussion	5	4	3	2	1

B. **Sessions**

Please indicate how useful each of the following were for you:

		Very much				Not at all
4.	Session 1 (Monday), topics 2-5 on introduction, demand for and sources of statistics, organization of statistical services	5	4	3	2	1
5.	Session 2 (Tuesday), topics 6-11 on basic principles of indicators, population, fertility and demonstration of calculating indicators	5	4	3	2	1
6.	Session 3 (Wednesday), topics 13-15 on education	5	4	3	2	1
7.	Session 4 (Thursday), topics 17-22 on economic activity, employment rural areas, time use and access to resources	5	4	3	2	1

		Very much				Not at all
8.	Session 5 (Friday), topics 25-30 on health, health services and nutrition, women's organizations and political participation	5	4	3	2	1
9.	Session 6 (Monday), field trip to Bindura	5	4	3	2	1
10.	Session 7 (Tuesday), topics 32-35, review of field trip, development of data bases and dissemination of indicators, policy and programme planning	5	4	3	2	1
11.	Small group calculation exercises	5	4	3	2	1

12. Comment on curriculum: _____

C. Seminar arrangements

Please indicate how satisfied you were with each of the following:

13.	Information received before the workshop	5	4	3	2	1
13a.	Workshop venue - Harare	5	4	3	2	1
14.	Travel arrangements	5	4	3	2	1
15.	Hotel accommodation	5	4	3	2	1
16.	Hotel meals/service	5	4	3	2	1
17.	Workshop staff	5	4	3	2	1

18. COMMENTS: _____

D. Seminar overall

19. What did you like best about the seminar?

    _____
    _____
    _____
    _____
    _____

20. What did you like least about the seminar?

    _____
    _____
    _____
    _____

21. What did you gain from the seminar?

    _____
    _____
    _____

22. What use do you think you will make of your experience at the seminar after its completion?

    _____
    _____
    _____

23. How could ECA/INSTRAW improve future seminars?

    _____
    _____
    _____

24. Please indicate what other kinds of seminars you would be interested in attending (if you check more than one, please indicate your first choice, second choice, etc.)

    _____ Development of proposals
    _____ Training in statistics/research techniques
    _____ General aspects of women in development
    _____ Other _____

Thank you for participating in the evaluation of this seminar.

Annex VI

DOCUMENTS DISTRIBUTED

1. D. Ahawo, "Development and dissemination of statistical indicators in Kenya with special reference to the status of women: A summary".

2. Food and Agriculture Organization of the United Nations, "The state of statistics on women in agriculture in the third world", by C. Safilios-Rothchild (ESA/STAT/AC.17/7-INSTRAW/AC.17/7).

3. _____ "Statistics and indicators on the role of women in agriculture and rural development", by D. C. Alonzo.

4. United Nations, Department of International Economic and Social Affairs, Statistical Office, and International Research and Training Institute for the Advancement of Women, "Background paper on statistics on economic activities with special reference to the situation of women", by Claes Norrlof.

5. _____ Compiling Social Indicators on the Situation of Women, Series F, No. 32 (United Nations publication, Sales No. E.84.XVII.2).

6. _____ Improving Concepts and Methods for Statistics and Indicators on the Situation of Women, Series F, No. 33 (United Nations publication, Sales No. E.84.XVII.3).

7. United States of America, Department of Commerce, Bureau of the Census, Women of the World. Sub-Saharan Africa, by Jeanne S. Newman, WID-2 (Washington, D.C., Government Printing Office, 1985).

8. Zimbabwe, Central Statistical Office, "Indicators for women's participation in development", by Gibson M. Mandishona.

9. _____ T. R. Nhongo, Minister of Community Development and Women's Affairs, Opening Address to the Seminar.